re-membering.

the heart of direct experience

re-membering

Important advisory:

As detailed in this book, a significant number of my most important life experiences have been afforded through the utility of various substances and practices. As much as I found these experiences immeasurably beneficial, I am well aware we are not all the same, there is nothing that can be assumed of the same productive utility for all. By way of example, there are many of us who struggle with the on-going re-percussions of prior negative events on our sensitive dispositions, re-percussions which for some may be exacerbated by engaging with the types of substances and practices such as I refer to here.

I find nothing shameful in feeling at times overwhelmed amid the memories of personal history's not so uncommon brutality. Such existential concern appears everyone's lot, with variability between individuals a matter of degree. Though knowledge of this human predicament serves only to motivate me further in the desire to aid individual efforts to liberate from the tyranny of such counterproductive mindsets and their often-on-going destructive consequences. At the same time, I sincerely respect there are limits to the degree of wholesome progress specific individuals may reasonably accomplish in this regard, especially when acting alone. For this reason, I wholeheartedly recommend seeking out the mentoring of those among us of the heart, mind and training appropriate to ably guide others through and beyond specific forms of obstructive encumbrance.

I add to this caveat a second, a response to a lesser concern stemming from a tendency of some to not take responsibility for their own choices. In this regard I will state the obvious, that I am in no way professionally qualified by way of societal institutions to be making recommendations of any kind. This book, after all, is simply a record of a life lived, complete with its reflections and ponderings. As much as I enjoy the benefit of the fruits of my findings and dis-coveries, as much as I see the potential benefit in reporting of and conversing about these with others, especially within a societal context of otherwise widespread, seemingly avoidable suffering in all its myriad and nuanced forms, the contents of this book still remain as of an authority similar to that of entries in a diary.

© 2022 by Joseph Quirk

All rights reserved. No part of this book may be reproduced in any form or by any means, electronic or mechanical, including photocopying, recording, or by any information storage and retrieval system, without permission in writing from the author.

quirkus111@gmail.com

If you find value of any kind within these pages, please share through recommending a reading to others. This not only disseminates that which you deem worthy, it also supports the author in contributing to the resources necessary to make such a work possible.

First Edition

Quirk, Joseph.

Re-membering (the heart of direct experience) / Joseph Quirk.

ISBN: 9798840916889

1. Self-knowledge   2. Tools and methods of awakening

3. Lifestyle design   4. Serendipity and synchronicity

5. Independence and tribalism   6. Institutional tyranny

re-membering

I dedicate these words to the very same individuals I acknowledge in contributing to their inspiration. This world is vastly populated with individuals whom in one way or another have played their part in the unfolding of my rich experience. From the people who live their lives in conventional ways and in doing so gift a resourceful platform upon which my opportunities continue to be afforded, through those who more directly act in contribution to the challenging interactions of my learning, to those who provide benevolent support at the times and places of most perceived need, for all of you, I have only gratitude. Without the sum of you this story could not be told.

I desire to especially acknowledge the contributions of my brothers jim, Steven Hepple and Paul Burrell. They were able to view my writing from a distance that I had not achieved personally, and thus provided invaluable feedback from matters of language to impressions regarding the content and flow of the story as a whole.

re-membering

[6]

re-membering

Table of contents

Preface	8
Introduction	10

Part 1: the driver

loosened moorings	17
despair and depression	43
the trail of scattered breadcrumbs	54
seclusion's revelations	99

Part 2: the vehicle

the bubble	125
activity and activism	139
the ancient continent and her unfamiliar inhabitants	161
music and mayhem	182
a much-maligned re-creation and her immeasurable benefits	215
re-membering	250

re-membering

Preface

I was never before inspired to write a book. The idea found sufficient traction only after decades of unusual and insightful experience met with a threshold accumulation of suggesting and prompting from respected long-term peers and the convenient circumstances of time and place. Before this confluence I had not considered my personal experiences of sufficient import to share of publicly, not in a world I understood to be already perfectly functioning in its accommodating of all inhabitant endeavours. Though that was an understanding arrived at without myself in the picture.

Conspicuously, my individual life experiences neatly coalesce into chapters. Rather than a co-incidence, this reflects the deliberate way in which I have differentiated my worldly activities. Beyond the emptiness I found on direct contact with traditional life pathways, beyond the renunciation of a life lived in accordance with the demands of others, and in recognition of the ease with which I could potentially lead myself astray, I determined to single-mindedly focus upon that which appeared the most important personal priority at the exclusion of all else. In this way I dedicated myself until novel experience sufficiently informed a re-evaluation of my chosen activity. This repeatedly led to re-prioritising, and thus to new chapters.

The disillusioning effect of experience upon prior established perceptions not only provided the opportunity for new outlooks to emerge, it also appeared as if to simultaneously re-model the world in accordance with new outlooks. A noticing of this pivotal role of perception re-volutionised the very way in which I approached subsequent priorities, shifting away from meaning-seeking into meaning-making, towards imaginative approaches to purposeful community involvement, through a complete makeover of personal presentation in the field of intimacy, ultimately arriving at something approximating a wilful engagement in all manner of activity with the spirit of playfulness.

Over time and through much experience, I came to realise perception as a powerfully creative self-fulfilling faculty. I more and more specialised my focus upon it, being the locus through which all experience finds its context. As this was a function over which I could maintain considerable creative control, I proceeded to less concern with that seemingly beyond my control, that being the shape in which worldly events tend to show up. This inner exercise then re-cognised emotion as a powerful ally, as an essential tool of navigation and informant of well-being. This alliance not only encouraged ventures into new territory, it also provided joy as a consistent companion regardless of the activity.

All this while I continuously encountered people suffering in uncountable ways at the hands of their own sub-conscious perspectives, their views and beliefs, their complexes. It is in re-spect of these social encounters I find motivation for the sharing of my dis-coveries, not because the subject matter to which I contribute is necessarily anything new, but because my contribution to the existing vast body of work perhaps provides a different angle, taking advantage of my uniqueness in reporting to the uniqueness of others. I understand my earliest of worldly impressions formed amid the conditions of a bygone era, during a broader period within which cultural evolution seems to pick up pace with each new iteration, though I am confident the principles and practices to which I share input are relevant to all modern humanity, uninhibited by the in-common world view changes that show up across multiple generations.

re-membering

Introduction

It is not entirely accurate to state this a work of non-fiction. Although it would be true to say the story is based on actual past events. Perhaps obviously, anecdotal reporting is always subject to the relative limits of personal perspective active at the time of referenced events, the questionable completeness of later re-collection, the modifying effects of subsequent experience on specific memories, and the influence of emotional disposition contemporary to re-call. As such, through the passage of time, evocations of previous happenings tend to take on the quality of ephemeral dreams. In any case, it feels imprudent and unnecessary to make any more concrete a claim regarding the factual basis of this composition.

The nebulous nature of memories has not at all bothered the writing. On the contrary, during the activity I have consistently sourced the delightful freedom that sits at the heart of uncompromising creative activity. I proceeded in the confidence that intrinsic value abides within the significance and consequence of specific life events, and not so much within a concern over the peripheral details and the accuracy of their subsequent recollection.

What this writing presents is a collation of happenings, insights and reflections. Principally, I offer all described within these pages as to document developments towards an unmistakable re-discovery, by way of honouring the essential and the wholesome, that which eludes any attempt at labelling or identification.

re-membering

The chain of events that led to this unlaboured uncovering exposed a world of wonder, in turn motivating a desire to contribute to the conversation on some of its major contributors and contributions. Of especial interest has been how the contents of this world are viewed and shaped through the philosophy of science, by the legacy of religion, as a consequence of general institutional taboo, within the consensus of society's herd dynamic, in the context of contrasting cultures, as experienced through the complexity of the human organism, as moderated through the insight of psychedelics, as assisted through the assurance of mentoring, as availed through the mystery of co-incidence, as directed through an undying call towards love and wisdom.

Specifically, this writing project began with a listing of all personal events deemed of potential interest and value to others. From there I set about threading these events together in a way that allowed for integration and flow, with an aim to render a consistently engaging narrative. I then added broader historical information as to provide context in areas felt of less likely familiarity to the reader. I kept this information general enough so as not to unnecessarily burden the storytelling, and so as not to digress to the point of moving into areas of non-fiction sufficiently reported on elsewhere.

The result of a reporting on life events only of perceived significance to a story is the portrayal of a life as edited. This may run the risk of misguiding the reader towards a sense of a life more brimming of adventures than is true to conclude. I can assure you my experiences have not been so consistently productive. My total life, as for most, is inclusive of much down time, of hesitations, of failures to act, of actions contrary to best interests, of self-sabotage, of old habituated ways, of ignorance, among much else. Though I have referred to less than fruitful episodes where relevant, I have limited such reporting in the interests of maintaining an engaging flow of eventful narrative development.

re-membering

re-membering

part 1

the driver

re-membering

re-membering

to take on views is inevitable

starting in infancy, through the years developed in complexity and descriptive detail

such views inform the senses and thus mould and define experience,

ultimately resulting in a world created

tho' all views are but perspectives, they speak of conditions and thus not of truths

as much as it is insisted on the contrary

upon this inherent subjectivity acknowledged,

how is it possible for such views to be seen for what they are, as incomplete and troublesome,

without at the same time eroding the very self-identity that developed in unison

and now seeks to understand?

how is this possible without dissolving the very world, the very place one calls home?

re-membering

loosened moorings

I recall my prior concern. I remember my desire to prepare for what may become a deeply troubling situation. Though how could I prepare for that which I had no prior experience nor reliable knowledge? How could I have made myself less vulnerable? It was to be either all in or nothing, I decided.

As it turned out the eventual encounter was not at all threatening, as much as it exposed the sub-conscious assumptions which hitherto formed the basis of my reality.

My mind had transitioned as to render sounds as dynamic objects immediately of three dimensions, at least three, perhaps more. This was as a physical environment, a soundscape. Initially my involvement within this space lacked specific focus, though once the mobility of my point of attention was understood, it encouraged an innate playfulness and curiosity, leading to more wilful and pointed exploration. The place was navigable. Upon investigation, these pre-recorded sounds were understood to be co-operative, in accord with my will, successively more prominent, and then less; louder, then softer; closer, then more distant. This place was interactive. It felt the space containing this audible phenomenon was of an infinite and timeless nature - infinite meaning this could be anywhere and thus potentially everywhere, though and thus no place in particular - timeless meaning at any time accessible, though only in the present. The happening appeared as other-worldly, and thus ultimately beyond explanation. This world normally lay hidden, obscured by the very conventional notions of time and place that provide the everyday its geometry.

This was not just some illusion, unless that is the nature of all occurrence, but then why single this experience out as such? Further, surely this is not something that merely relates to sound, for if sounds may be so amenable, so personalised, then what of the nature of all else perceptible through the senses? And what of reality as summarily referenced, as insisted upon as something external, objective, and thus the same for all? I was not co-orchestrating the quantity and quality of these sounds for all. For others surely the experience would be different and potentially equally radically unique.

Upon reviving a sense of time and its passing, my social impulse reared. I carefully lifted the needle from the record to which I had been listening, turned off the amplifier, and proceeded downstairs to re-join my comrades. In my absence the guys had enthusiastically decided on a trip to the local fast-food drive through. They shared a craving, a mutual case of the munchies.

We had gathered at my family's house for this, my first experience with marijuana. My companions had tried it once before. Most notable was the occasion of their meeting in the forest inhabiting one side of our school's sports fields. On that afternoon one within the loose collective panicked upon feeling the effects of the smoked buds, prompting him to hurry from the cover of trees towards the residence of the Christian Brothers who dished out our daytime education. As a reaction to the boy's request for assistance, the police were called. A story ended up in the city's most popular newspaper regarding the event, lending the occasion widespread notoriety.

Outcomes like this served as a reminder of the then state of our relationship with all authority figures. The boy was asking for help. Instead he was apprehended. There was no consideration that perhaps someone with medical skills or of relevant welfare experience may be of better service. As a rule, adults were not our friends. Neither did they act in the way of elders in the archaic sense. There was no evidence of love nor wisdom. It was all essentially a repetitive regime of coercion. Teachers and clergy, parents and police, all took part in an uneasy co-alition.

This inspired my rebellion. I was unwilling to perform as an empty vessel to such callous external command. This manner of treatment directly violated my innate sense of freedom. It was the uneasy deliberations regarding the potential risk of being caught by these authorities and the likely consequences that led to my decision not to participate in that first outing.

This time around, in the absence of my parents, I considered the family home to be sufficiently safe for a first experience. Houses of this era and location were built as strongholds against the prying eyes of outsiders. It was as if the community lived permanently in fear of some looming external threat. In this suburban location even neighbours were held in suspicion. After five years of occupation we remained non-acquainted with the majority of those that lived beyond the boundary hedges and across the wide tarmac. With doors locked and curtains strategically drawn it was very unlikely we would be disturbed nor our activity discovered.

The rolled foil, the size of a small cigar, had been carefully opened, a joint not so expertly, but effectively rolled. No sooner had it been lit, passed around, and inhaled, had the effect been realised. It was swift, clean and immense. It felt as to immediately transmogrify all previously known mundane phenomena into animate existence. It was like a mist had cleared. It was like waking up from a sleep into a dream. I felt as to be bathing in the presence of all things.

This awareness and my subsequent explorations became totally consuming. Nature spoke to me of and about itself. Life existed everywhere, not just where science says it is. It dwelled within the very fabric of all phenomena. I was drawn to the most glistening of light spectacles visible through a slight parting of the curtains above the kitchen sink. If not for the concern of drawing unwanted neighbourly attention and the likelihood of its negative judgments, murmurings, and re-actions, I would have moved outdoors to immerse myself amongst the blades of grass and within the breeze that continued in its voicing of pre-history through its rustling of the eucalypt leaves.

The munchies expedition sounded too much, an unnecessary addition to the already hyper-stimulating goings-on. The momentum among the group, however, cared not for debate. In wishing to remain in company, and for the sake of the brotherhood, I decided to join them. My heart increased its rate of beating accordingly.

In suburban Brisbane, as in all suburban environs and for most activities, the plan meant a drive in the car. I took a back seat, a suitable berth for one along for the ride. The two friends who occupied the front seats chattered and giggled loudly. The sudden powerful roar of the engine was startling, six cylinders of exploding harmony. The automatic addition of music from the vehicle's considerable rear speakers filled the interior with a further layer of visceral vibration. There was much going on, too much to trouble with through considering consequence. I let go of any such attempt at interpretation, and settled into the state of nervous energy now traversing my body.

The streets and roads that linked us to the local burger drive-through were devoid of people. It was always rare to see pedestrians. The prevailing culture had no time for aimless wandering, only designated activities were accepted as normal. It was not enough to be without purpose. Everything required at least one reason. Residents were mustered from the confines of their fortress-like abodes, to their enclosed places of work or study, to equally constrained, appropriately-named shopping complexes, less often to sporting venues of a specific code or to a church of a specific denomination, all achieved through the agency of the enclosed vehicle. Beyond this people did not mingle much. They kept within their small affiliations, fed by frequent dramatised television media and circulating social gossip.

On our journey the lads were given to regular bouts of uncontrollable laughter, especially Dave, the vehicle owner and driver. In the midst of a single outburst he would inhale without ceasing his hysterics, leading to a temporary stark modulation, the result I could only compare to the emanation of a walrus pup. Pulling up at the drive-through did not quell the outpouring. On the contrary, the incision of the young female voice through the speaker at the service entrance provoked in an even higher level of raucousness.

"May I take your order?" she enquired as may a robot.

I was in no doubt that she could, but was unsure whether the boys could actually deliver one. I felt uneasy with the unnecessary attention we were attracting. Had my school friends not learned from their ordeal with the police only a month previous? Only Mark, who shared the back seat, appeared to be displaying much additional concern. Though he was delivering a mixed message, incredulity, mild distress, abandonment.

The exchange was eventually negotiated, something I did not take for granted. How do we manage to keep it all together? How does society as a whole manage to function with all its increasing complexity and scale, constituted out of the totality of all such micro-interactions among such inconsistent human functioning? I'm well aware of my own faltering inconsistencies. To multiply this out to the millions, and then get it to work is beyond impressive. If proof was sought for the existence of miracles, then there it was, in plain sight.

After returning home, after the fast food had been devoured, I noticed that my previous clarity and sensitivity had significantly diminished. A burger had dulled me. I suspected a significant part of my energy was now focused on the digestion of food. It was then and there I decided to ignore any appetite for food during such sessions in the future. There was too much to explore, process, and allow to inform my understanding to so carelessly forego the opportunity. As for my comrades, there was no evidence they were at all of similar mind. Nothing was mentioned, and to look at them was to procure no such sign. Their busy behaviour was more indicative of minds distracted from any such concern.

I did not relate anything of my experiences to anyone. Such revelations did not form part of what was ever discussed, with peers or anyone else. I felt any mention would rather be met with disbelief and mockery. This type of reaction dissuaded all but the narrowest of impersonal routine conversational assertions at that time. It characterised a general lack of depth in all relationships. This absence of sincere relating felt increasingly limiting. Surely I was not the only one who felt this way, yearning to validate personal experience as of substance. I did not know because I never asked. To do so would have been to risk greater social isolation. The alternative was to feel more alone. Paradoxically, this increased reliance on the group for company, though without much of a sense of what bound us together. The sum of us made for a fragile community, vulnerable to the roughshod dealings of surrounding officialdom and exploitation at the hands of individuals of less scrupulous motivation.

∞

That first experience into the nature of sound was to be my first lead towards a life of meaning. Though I could not claim it as a prescription for informing my day to day operations as the nature of my discovery was so slippery and ephemeral. Previous to that occurrence I had really only known meanings as parts of structured meta-narratives - a story of an omnipotent creator in which I was required to believe through the agency of a church, along with the seemingly juxtaposed tale of life success defined in terms of material acquisition. My recent personal encounter did not provide for such comparatively easy conceptualisations. Neither did it comfortably sit within these pre-existing ones. Conversely, the inhaling of the smoke of a plant's buds had singularly and directly cast doubt on the foundations of these formerly conditioned ideologies. My direct agency in co-creating how sound is experienced spoke of a relationship with creation and creator most intimate. In the same instance, the proclaimed material world did not appear so material. In fact, it presented as much more elusive, something to be negotiated, something not so easily accumulated, and even less so, successfully coveted.

The insight I gained through the auspices of the marijuana plant had vindicated my search beyond my conditioned culture. It had provided an inspiration through which to propel my life forward. This had now become the only truth I knew. I recognised it as truth because it was directly experienced. It played out within and exposed the nature of my relationship with the world. This felt as the undeniably appropriate measure of truth. Any life of value surely must respect this nature if it was to have any integrity. To exist without such reverence is surely to be lost within a web of ideas, concepts, abstractions, that which has no life.

At the time I did not question so much of why the ingesting of such an informative natural herb was prohibited. I was simply motivated to find out more to further my own experience. This impelled me to seek out the company of people with which I could share openly regarding such findings. Perhaps there were whole communities dwelling beyond my present social circles offering a way of life that aligned with such direct personal insights. I had no idea of where this may lead, but indeed it was my only lead.

∞

Despite the apparent distance I felt separated my friends and myself in terms of interests and direction, we still shared a desire for adventure, escaping the reach of those who sought to force upon us a life of apparent slavery. In the months that followed, excursions were planned including trips that took us beyond the borders of our home territory. Brisbane at the time existed without the modern-day standard addition of the city bypass. All traffic was required to slow down within city limits.

As my parent's residence was located an easy walk from the highway as it exited the city to the south, the situation lent itself to our service. Lacking transport of our own, it provided the potential for hitchhiking.

The first time I tried this was with two other, by this time, former school companions. We stood at a spot under adequate street lighting just beyond a major intersection and just beyond midnight. Any suggestion of inappropriate timing for such an activity was quickly and easily eclipsed by the enthusiasm of escape from the familiarity of restrictions into the freedom of the unknown. We took turns in standing on the curb and extending one arm with thumb pointing in our direction of travel in keeping with convention. Within the hour we had secured our first ride, a semi-trailer. These largest of vehicles shed bright light on the road ahead, granting the driver ample opportunity to spot us and ponder the choice of offering a lift while he waited for the intersection lights to turn green.

Some minor skill and focus were required to co-ordinate the hoist of our backpacks and the climb into the cabin. The interior of the vehicle was surprisingly spacious. The area behind the seats included a raised bunk, a place to rest for the driver on long hauls. It was here I perched, exciting with imaginings of what may lay ahead. The darkness that shrouded the truck's cabin further enhanced a sense of mystery. The only significantly bright illumination shone out from the headlights onto the next 50 metres of road. I was oblivious to any danger, contrary to the warnings of my protective upbringing. I was happy to trust the occasion.

This first time out and about was not so much directed to any specific destination. It was more motivated simply by the desire of getting away. The highway runs roughly parallel with the shape of the natural coastline to the east. During that era the coastline attracted much of the urban development, while to the west, much of the lowlands had been claimed for cattle grazing, with mountainous areas left aside for regeneration and conservation. Over the following days we tended to the west, visiting small rural townships and camping in parks and fields before looping back in the direction of our home of habit. Without knowing at the time, I suppose this was more of a pilot mission, a reconnaissance. It granted us more of an understanding of what was possible in terms of destinations. It allowed us to explore the lay of the land and examine the viability of hitchhiking as a reliable means of transport. The results were encouraging.

On future excursions, attempts were made to get going well before dark. There are obviously more vehicles on the road during this time, with drivers more likely to offer a ride within the greater relative safety of the sunlit hours. This in turn minimised longer waits and maximised the chance of arrival at what became more and more a predetermined destination at a time convenient for organising and settling in without a problem. Our destination of choice invariably became Nimbin, home of the Aquarius Festival, Australia's mini-Woodstock. Since the inaugural festival the village had become the centre of the country's counter-culture, a culture that highly valued cannabis and other psychedelics as part of a more holistic lifestyle.

Within the Nimbin area, as for Australia generally, there were black inhabitants prior to white settlement. There is conjecture regarding how long the black fellas have actually occupied this part of the continent, though oral tradition maintains this time as at least 12 000 years. Specifically, the Bundjalung Nation occupied a region within which Nimbin is located close to its northern extremity. 'Nation' is the term used to describe this community of people because before British colonisation over 500 distinct peoples and languages existed across the continent, and thus each formed its own independent society. The name Nimbin originated from the local language within which the word 'Nimbinjee' refers to the spirits that protect the area.

Reportedly, when white man arrived, he did not acknowledge the black fellas as land owners. Australia was deemed by the new arrivals to be there for the taking. The British concluded there had been no land under cultivation, and thus, there existed no evidence of civilised people. This argument was aptly summarised by the Latin phrase 'Terra nullius' meaning nobody's land. In the Nimbin area white settlers came first for the timber, and when returns diminished, land was cleared for dairy farming where convenient to do so. This industry, in turn, collapsed in the 1960s due to a declining demand for its products. In 1973, the Aquarius Festival became the first event in the entire country to recognize traditional black ownership, and sought permission for the use of land for the event from the Bundjalung elders. It was those that remained after the festival, students, hippies and party-goers, who made up the core of what was to become the newest addition to the Nimbin community.

I arrived into the mix some 8 years later. I had set off with Steve and Mark, two of the co-conspirators in my first experience with ganja. A utility vehicle provided an open tray upon which we sat, backs against the rear cabin window, looking out upon a passing landscape lit by a setting sun. The situation prompted a rich insinuation as to what freedom may look and feel like. Perhaps only the act of casting away amongst the cargo on a slow-moving train could have carried more metaphorical intensity.

It was getting dark as we closed in on our destination. Our host had offered to drop us in Nimbin village at a later time if we were agreed to a prior brief diversion. He described this stopover as a men's meeting, a gathering of Christians for the purpose of worship. For my part I nodded with a mixture of gratitude, respect, humour, fatalism, and the recognition of the convenience that a little patience may bring. The meeting was held in a small hall in a forest still some 50 kilometres shy of our destination. The hall was of a common design from a previous era, providing utility for whatever purpose the community may deem useful. The single room with its adjoining kitchen area became punctually filled with quite a young group of males.

Soon the formalities got underway amidst salutations, expressions of personal veneration, and group prayers. The proceedings quickly stirred up feelings of agitation within me. My immune system kicked in. I had been brought up amid an earlier iteration of this religious practice and had developed an aversion. In this situation, however, I was an outsider, and this afforded me some distance. I still felt disheartened. It was as if these men had given up on their potential to operate freely and openly in the world. It was as if being who they were was not enough. But if all are made of or by a god then why the need for exclusive membership amongst a privileged few? How does this assist in the embracing of all as of one divine origin?

I wished to leave behind this singing of praise for a creator which I did not know nor believed existed in the form implied through the behaviour of these men. I exchanged glances with my comrades through which we sufficiently communicated a consensus to move outside. Once out and under the trees I felt free of the pressure of unwanted conformity. I felt relaxed within my own church, in the home of my own admiration, that of the magnificence of nature.

Soon after finding a spot sufficiently distant from the hall, Mark produced a joint to share. By the time it was just about exhausted, a member of the men's gathering, the passenger in the utility vehicle that had delivered us, emerged from the building and walked towards us.

"Have you been smoking devil's weed?" he asked in a disapproving tone.

To answer in the affirmative would be to admit to involvement in some type of demonic activity, a negative response would be to lie. My hands felt momentarily tied.

"It was him!" Steve responded in light comical relief, raising a finger in Mark's direction.

I released a loud laugh, which in turn facilitated the relaxing of my sphincter. I appreciated Steve's playful wittiness in rebuffing the accusation, albeit at the expense of our long-term friend and traveling companion. Understandably neither Mark nor our host were amused. Regardless, the conversational tone soon settled and nothing further came of the exchange. It appeared Steve had successfully diffused any intensity. I felt free to further enjoy the company of the trees.

We approached Nimbin village from the south on a road that wound its way through a landscape of continuous small rolling hills. Ambient moonlight provided sufficient illumination to clearly make out mountain peaks immediately to the west. The occasional extruding sheer rock face stood in proclamation of the power of the area's ancient volcanic past. As the panoramic views and our speed diminished, the increasing density of human settlement provoked dialogue in equal measure. There were now cultural icons that represented the familiar. Their accumulated meaning formed part of our shared but limited world view, even in this place to which I had not previously visited. The town hall, the pub, the church, the cafes and park, all were familiar, all represented institutions suggestive of how we were to conduct ourselves.

Our hosts pulled up in the village centre, just before the road forked to the north and the east. This placed our options in clear sight. After jumping down from the rear of the vehicle and thanking our conveyor, we made short work of deciding on where to proceed. We made our way to what was most familiar among the familiar. We entered the pub, ordered beers, and sat down.

All chapters of Nimbin's ancient to recent past were represented among the humans gathered, though each to their own, down to the last customer, divided. A group of black fellas sat quietly around a round table, next to a window that looked out upon the street. A line of farmers lined the bar, obvious by their uniforms of heavy duty. So called hippies, dressed in their own kind of uniform of long hair, bare feet and loose draping clothes, occupied the most space, from the veranda that looked out upon the mountains to the east through to the dimly-lit and carpeted lounge further to the interior.

Where is the commonality among these disparate populations of humanity? My self-consciousness provoked this most obvious yet uncomfortable of questions. This was not a query entertained out of philosophical novelty nor something motivated in a hunt for good will. It was not prompted by the eye. It had arisen in reaction to the felt atmosphere. The extent to which each sub-culture presented with a level of stifled posturing mirrored as a tension within my self. That tension, as tension does, sought release.

Viewing the problem hypothetically, it was easy to superimpose a narrative of loose fit. Historically, the often-violent exchanges that ultimately led to the taking away of previously free-ranging land from the black fellas would be enough for them to feel their home had been devastatingly compromised. Based upon the little I had learned, for these people cultural meaning rose from an inseparable connection with the land, with country. In the absence of unconditional access, what of life's integrity remains? Here they sit as offspring to those originally trespassed upon and severed, in the same room as representatives from among the present majority holders of these lands, now divided and parcelled.

Do these farmers feel anything regarding the plight of the black fellas? Perhaps something lies deeper under the surface, unconscious beneath the constancy of physical activity, the concerns of day to day affairs. Separate individuals, separate land and resources, unitary input costs and bottom lines, competitive markets, abstract isolating notions in stark contrast to the culture of the inhabitants who preceded them. The predicament of the white settler appears immediately and equally troubling in its very invocation of fragmentation, uncertainty and struggle.

For the hippies, as for I, mainstream society with its concerns was something to be avoided. Subsidised through the affluence of parents and a social welfare system delivered on the back of an urgent post-war extractive economy, preoccupied within the exploration of mind and experience, questions of greater community cohesion rarely arose. To drop out was a common slogan of this section of the era's children. Sure, 'love' was a common enough word in the hippy vocabulary, but its application appeared to relate more to that which arises intimately between newly adopted brothers and sisters.

Where is the commonality among these disparate populations of humanity? Is a resolution of tensions possible? Is this even the right question? Perhaps the very notion of community harmony is merely an abstract utopian ideal. Does not a harmonious society require a common story, a consensus of what the world is or means, and thus of what may constitute an appropriate relationship within it? I cannot truly speak from experience for how others perceive their surrounds and therefore neither can I speak of their relationships. In this context, all others are but characters within my own life's unfolding. So is this my problem? From where does my own social dis-ease originate? Is there a way in which I may accept the state of human affairs without feeling a need to try and fix it?

Whatever this society's recent colonial past, to maintain open awareness within full view of its brutal consequence requires a strong will and heart. To additionally question its functioning is almost too much to contemplate. Most parties present appear to wish to forget. Alcohol may well play an appropriate role to anesthetise against any such thought-filled distractions.

Closing time was upon us. Customers were organising more alcohol to be taken away to further their inebriation. Having gathered our packs, we made our way to the footpath and looked around for signs of activity that may further our evening's objectives. Our first priority was to score some buds, to purchase some weed. There was a substantial number of hippies making their way across the road and into what appeared to be a café. The entrance door was closed; however, people were passing inside and then shutting the door behind them. We decided to follow.

The interior was already crowded. The majority of those gathered were seated along long bench tables. There was the pungent smell of ganja. Large plumes of smoke hung in the air. Soon after taking a seat near to the entrance, a very large joint was passed our way. We helped ourselves to a few puffs before passing it on. A plate of mushrooms soon followed as an offering. Having never experienced the effects of these gold-topped fungi, I declined, leaving it for a time in which I was a little more secure in my surrounds to explore what insights they may offer.

A bearded musician came and sat on a small stage to the rear of the room. He began to play familiar songs, songs that had emerged through the peak of the American hippy movement of the late '60s. The music increased the levels of joyful human voice within the room, seducing me to rise above the concerns I had entertained in the pub earlier.

Another joint came my way. I asked the provider if there was any possibility of buying. This man turned to his companion, and after a brief conversation between them, relayed a message back to wait where I was. The two men left the gathering, and returned shortly after. One of them indicated to join them outside, and accordingly, my companions and I filed out. We followed to the nearest shop front, closed and dark at this time of night, but designed with a recessed entranceway that provided some cover from vicarious viewing.

Their offering was presented in a disposable plastic household garbage bag. It was about half full. We had not intended to purchase such a huge amount. I smiled incredulously at my companions, and in quiet voices we discussed whether this was for us. Not knowing if we would be conveniently offered further untroubled transactions, we decided to agree to the purchase, expensive for us, though affordable. I was only just able to stuff the bag into my large, mostly empty backpack.

After this successful deal we agreed the next priority was to safeguard our hoard and look for a haven within which to sleep for the night. We had completed our mission in good time, though we had as yet no idea where we would set up camp. It was getting on towards midnight.

We took the fork out of town to the north and headed in the direction of the distant mountains. This road crossed a beautiful stream where an old wooden factory stood beside the babble of the flowing waters. As we passed out of the small village, the absence of street lighting allowed for a clear moon-lit view of the mountains. The peaks were shrouded in clouds. The whole scene stimulated my imagination to mystical proportions. Immersed in this enchanted dream-like landscape I was in no hurry to go anywhere. I had already arrived. Timelessness again became my companion.

Practically speaking, it's not that we had far to go. We only needed to find a site which provided sufficient privacy from the road and level ground to set up tents, a situation unlikely to be discovered by undesirable intrusion before the next day became light. Soon a suitable area came into view inside a barbed wire fence running parallel to the road. We acknowledged that barbed wire meant cows, but were sufficiently at ease knowing these animals were generally mild creatures, uninterested in any sort of confrontation. We threw our gear over the fence, taking it in turns to hold the wires apart in order to allow our mutual passing without jagging our clothing on the barbs. We then made our way into the paddock to a distance sufficient to obscure the road. It is here we set up our tents. It was here I passed into peaceful sleep.

∞

These early hitchhiking adventures coincided with the beginning of my time at university. The accompanying sudden expansion in freedom was further enhanced as a result of my parents' surprising decision on a move to Papua New Guinea. My father had been offered a significant promotion within the bank to which he committed most of his waking life's time and energy. No doubt my parents subjected themselves to considerable worried deliberation before ultimately deciding the package too good to refuse. It meant a large rise in my father's wage and substantial fringe benefits, but it also meant leaving their three oldest sons behind in habitation of the family home.

So soon after my emancipation from the comprehensively imposed restrictions of my youth, through the re-moval of my parents, I had been left to sharing of a large house in circumstances devoid of regulation. To go from a strict regime of school, church, church youth group and nothing else in terms of permitted social outings, to a situation within which all is possible, optional and unsupervised, is at once a great personal opportunity for adventure and misadventure, and a prescription for disappointment of parental and societal expectations.

Social opportunities expanded through university connections and previous school acquaintances. Sean, a year younger, became my closest of confidents. In him I had found someone of similar fascination on a broad range of subjects. Never really short of conversation, we saw many a night through within the sanctuary of the large family fortress. Some of Sean's friends attended a nearby university that specialised more in the humanities and the natural sciences. These schools attracted individuals pursuant of interests more directly personal, in lifestyle, philosophy, alternative perspectives, less about career and societal status. This cohort further entertained curiosity for exploring the mind's potential through the use of psychedelics. This university's location within a forest, and its provision of chemistry laboratories and on-campus student residences presented as an ideal environment for experimentation. I was soon granted an opportunity to benefit from these circumstances.

∞

What I first noticed out of the ordinary were the colours the girl was adding to a rainbow-like pattern on her page in how they began to intensify. Soon after the colours proceeded to glow and then run off the page. This was mesmerising and drew me in to the minute detail. The previously almost childlike drawing had now become, not only an object of beauty, it had come to life. Upon peering at the face of the female artist, she too had morphed from a formerly rather non-descript figure to a female of angelic and ageless beauty. The situation had become intense, though not alarmingly so. Nothing felt threatening. All felt benevolent.

This was the beginning of an experience in the effects of what had been assuredly offered as LSD (Lysergic acid diethylamide), or simply 'acid.' Acid can be procured in a colourless liquid form, though it is more commonly supplied in measured individual doses absorbed within small squares of cardboard for the purpose of convenient transport, distribution and ingestion. Assurance gained through known integrity or trustworthiness through the supply chain is recommended. Otherwise bad actors may potentially supply irregular dosage, a different harmful substance or nothing at all absorbed within the cardboard. Even if all parties engage in good faith, the experience remains uncertain as the effects in sufficient dose may completely dissolve the everyday. The trip can be mind-blowing.

Although able to be synthesised, acid is a chemical that occurs naturally in ergot, a fungus known historically to commonly colonise rye grain in the field. As has often been the case throughout the history of discovery in general, the effect of acid on humans was reportedly happened upon by accident. As the story goes, the chemical was inadvertently ingested by a Swiss scientist while working on other unrelated medical applications of the ergot fungus during the earlier part of the twentieth century. This man is suggested to have been the first to identify the chemical in its connection with altered mind states, although there is strong evidence suggesting this was not the first time humanity had inadvertently come in contact with LSD's psychoactive effects.

Records from the Salem witch trials of 1692-93 describe a pair of young girls exhibiting strange and severe physical symptoms, along with convulsions and reported hallucination. Through the prevailing lens of puritanical religiosity of the time, the girls were diagnosed as bewitched, set upon by demonic forces. The spread of similar symptoms through the community led to the rounding up and execution of some 20 females accused of witchcraft. It has been more recently acknowledged ergot grew on the rye grain cultivated and consumed within these communities, and the symptoms displayed by the girls as reported within the trial records have been suggested as of for ergotism.

I had arrived at the university residence for the experience along with Sean, though he had since disappeared. As the effects began to intensify, I sought his company for support. I left the bedroom where I had been observing that girl and that drawing. I took a seat on the edge of a sofa in the lounge room where two further young females were watching tennis on the television.

I followed the ball on the screen, feeling it was something through which I could ground myself. The ball became two, and then more. At a rate faster than I could follow, the number of balls crossing the net continued to multiply, their paths no longer able to be easily followed. I turned away. Soon one of the girls changed the channel, although the pair didn't appear particularly intent on the TV. They talked between themselves in a larger-than-life way suggesting they too were tripping.

I began to focus again on the screen. There were a couple of American soldiers patrolling through jungles that appeared to be of South-East Asia. I quickly and seamlessly found myself walking behind them on full alert. Suddenly a tiger appeared, and we turned around and ran, beating our way through thick vegetation. We soon arrived at a river and a departing boat in enough time to scramble aboard. Further along the river we happened upon the vessel of a fishing family. The soldiers became anxious, one was especially paranoid these locals may be concealing weapons. As one of the fishers moved to reach for something within a concealed basket, this soldier set off a panicked reaction leading to all members of the fishing boat being killed in a spray of bullets.

"Can't you see what you're doing?" the officer in charge screamed!

"Yeeeeesss!" I cried in reaction, acknowledging I had brought these circumstances upon myself. I had taken the acid, and through doing so brought these circumstances upon myself.

re-membering

The girls sitting in the lounge turned and looked, having the effect of re-embodying me within the room. I started to dry retch.

"Looks like he's having a bad trip," one said to the other in a tone suitable to that of a detached but curious onlooker.

At the time I lacked sufficient grounding to explain my outburst, to appease their concerns. I did not feel I was having a bad trip. I did not feel there was anything toxic within the substance I had ingested. The circumstances had become briefly terrifying, and I understood my reaction given the situation. I had now escaped that fate, though everything remained intense. There was nothing normal, and thus nothing that I could relate to, nothing that life as I had previously known it reasonably relied upon. The girls were now caricatures within my animation. What sustained me was this continuing sense this happening was of a benevolent nature. Away from the TV screen, all that arose had its genesis in the prevailing architecture. This I felt I could negotiate.

Physically I remained strong. I did not feel drunk, nor even dizzy. I simply struggled to make sufficient sense of my surroundings in order to function normally. Nothing remained still sufficient to orient myself in advance. All was in motion. If I could just focus then I could achieve regular functioning, I thought. The rate at which I was bombarded by my own attempts at control was disabling. I felt I needed to completely let go in order to achieve some form of stasis, and this needed to be executed at the point of origin of these seeming internal auto-suggestions. This presented as a paradox. I was attempting to prevent my own engagement through the action of my own engagement.

Mindful of this conundrum I sought a space where the objective could perhaps be attended to more easily. I stumbled to the front door of the residence. I managed to open the door. I then slowly descended the stairs with the assistance of the railing. Finding myself outside allowed movement into the open spaces of, of, of … what?

The path that led out from the building rose and fell in symmetrical peaks and troughs. The undulation of the path was active. It was moving like a ribbon blowing in the breeze. I looked up as a strong wind blew amidst the tree tops, entraining the branches that now rubbed against each other, creating a clear brushing sound. The trees were tropical palms, coconut palms. At regular intervals military helicopters flew low across the top of them. These were of a make appropriate to the war movie I had just walked out of. I wasn't sure if it was the helicopters creating the wind. Everything appeared to be moving as one.

I began to glide along the path. In short time I had begun to let go into the experience. Being alone and amongst nature allowed me the time and space to relax. I felt into my surrounds and engaged less with thoughts. Thoughts became less frequent and less perturbing as they passed through, their nature felt less personal. It felt composing to walk. It was something I could do without confusion. I walked and walked and walked and walked and walked and walked and walked.

I reminded myself this is a psychedelic trip, a hallucination, and thus it would be of limited duration and impact. The network of paths was extensive. I found joy within this activity. I could continue as much as I desired. The way I chose joined a more stationary vehicular access which caused me to become a little more self-conscious. Though I was soon able to exit this road as another pedestrian path appeared to exit away from the university precinct. This path began to ascend. Steps appeared. I slowed. As I approached a summit the steps ceased and the flat path re-emerged. I was no longer singularly keen on walking. I imagined myself resting. Once reaching the peak I moved to a place where I could enjoy a view.

Through a break in the trees I was just able to make out the scenery below. It was starting to become light. I could make out domes in the distance and dust rising under the hooves of donkeys driven along unpaved thoroughfares. I was looking down upon India.

re-membering

This scene I was keen to explore, however there was no path down that side of the mountain. To break trail felt potentially troublesome, if not dangerous. My other options were to return in the direction from which I had come or descend a sealed road that wound its way to the east. As I was not one for return journeys, I continued on the sealed road.

The further I descended, the more the environment and my functioning returned to the familiarity of normalcy.

∞

I did not require this experience. I already knew of perception as negotiable. What I did not know was that the mundane could be so comprehensively transformed. During the trip, normal phenomena had existed as mere tethering points around which the imagination played. As magnanimously wonderful as it became, all manifestation still appeared only within the limiting extremes of the meaningful. The unfolding wave-like repetitions pulsed with unerring frequency either side of the familiar. The experience could only find analogy in dreams. Within my entire history of waking states, I recall no such equivalent.

The experience generated no troubling after effects, beyond the further doubting and investigation of what is at all other times endlessly demanded upon as reality. It was not solely my assisted experiences that drew me into such fundamental questioning. What was more concerning to this end was society's insistent ravings. If something is real, or true, then surely there is no need to labour the point. Integrity is established through the ability to stand, not through unremitting assertion. Further, knowledge of truth is reflected in a knower's ease of exposition, not in their urgency. This felt incongruence was the greater part of my motivation to suspicion.

Of course, I could accept the need for a degree of pragmatic consensus commensurate with a harmonious co-operation among society's many players. This affords any system a degree of stability, a reliable foundation for an individual's endeavours within the community. Though the prevailing consensus appeared to be overstated well beyond its utility, rendering an ice-like solidity to what may be otherwise healthily negotiated, rather enjoyed much like as a fluid, as with the nature of water.

∞

The abundance of marijuana sourced from the trip down south allowed me to supply others with the opportunity to enjoy and perhaps learn from its experience. This turned into a reasonable earner for me. However, the activity came with responsibilities, interactions became negotiations, the atmosphere that of a market place. Friends and acquaintances surprised me with their discernment, their questioning of quantity and quality. Scales were needed for accurate measurement and reputational integrity. Requests increased more and more as the word got out through friends, and friends of friends, ….

One evening there came an unexpected knock on the door. The noise was comparatively loud, suggesting some assumed authority on the part of the visitor. I sat up and quickly scanned my mind for who this might be, though came up blank. The TV was already advertising my presence so I felt better than to ignore the intrusion.

After gathering my attention, I made my way to the door and answered with caution. The character standing there under the entrance light was someone I had not seen since my school days. A former fellow student who had been a trouble maker with a reputation for fighting. I heard he had more recently enrolled in the army from which he had proceeded to go AWOL. In my desire to get rid of him I feigned the disappointment of having no weed to sell. He briefly held his ground, staring as if into my eyes, all the while maintaining his trademark fixed grin. Thankfully he turned and left without prompting any further requirement for response.

I slowly closed and locked the door, though felt no more secure. I stood in the hallway immobile, dumbfounded. This visitation triggered an alternative interpretation, a re-imagining of my current lifestyle within my mind, one populated with the cold indifference of shady actors and the suspicious screaming accusations of the vicarious on-looker, the prying, resentful, vindictive all too common man.

re-membering

despair and depression

"I can play better than that shit!"

I must have sounded pathetic. Even from my own perspective it was pathetic. It was as much a cry for help. I admit there was something deeply wrong. Slumped in the semi-darkness, by myself as was my want, I eyed off, albeit askance and askew, the lone guitarist-singer. I didn't care how pathetic I looked as I no longer held respect for the views of others.

At first it was only adult authority figures that attracted my contempt, but now it was getting scary. It was slowly dawning the alliances which had lent courage to my rebelliousness, the associations which fuelled my sense of direction and purpose into my early 20s were not founded on any lasting integrity. For those I had presumed as comrades, our prior activities were now rather appearing as of the nature of an adolescent front, one that only served to obscure an underlying accumulating world view that re-presented the materialist values inherited by the previous generation. I had assumed without evidence the aim of my peers was to endure in defiance of the prevailing edifice, but when the responsibility of an independent life choice became relevant, their previous conduct appeared no longer tenable. There was now comparatively little to subsidise it, and so it became an inconvenience. What remained was a collection of habits prevailing for the inadvertent purpose of mere ritualised nostalgia. For my cohort our previous activities were not intended to lead to a life alternative to which had been prescribed and imposed. It never presented as a way out and beyond. Had any of us been paying attention?

I was alone in a crowd. Even at this inner-city bar, I had been accompanied, but felt and was left alone. It was as if they knew, or at least were not so insensitive as to ignore my evasive behaviour. No one attempted to help, my feeling was clearly none of them could, and I hated them for it. I did not want to be alone, but there was no-one with which I felt I could reasonably and usefully share regarding my dilemma. I was in crisis at age 21.

∞

I trace the origins of this emergency back to the final year of my compulsory schooling. Although really this is somewhat arbitrary. Is there a truly definitive beginning to anything, one that could allow reason to figure? Clearly not, as if there was then all could be surely resolved. There could be calculable answers to life's most important questions, simply through the tracing and remedying of original cause.

On a day close to the end of my senior year, I stood in the toilets on the ground floor of the building that included my home classroom, not that my classroom was at all homely. This place where we managed out excreta was a little more like home or at least somewhere we could call ours, even amid its atmosphere of wall to wall stinking acridity.

A large inhale on my cigarette did not serve to clarify my predicament. I gazed at a piece of paper that represented a potential future, a commitment to potentially more of the same. It was an application form for university entrance. It questioned my preferences for on-going study. I justify this moment as critical because it was the first time I had ever paused to ponder my future. Oh, my life? Yes, it is mine. After 18 years I knew little about it.

I had no idea of what to do. I just felt the need to decide within a rapidly diminishing period of time. One well-engrained reaction to any questioning by authority had been to tell them what I felt they wanted to hear. Not to do so was to provoke wrath and derision, and end up in no better place for it.

At times I did not co-operate in this game, though in the context of the classroom setting, such objections were sometimes met with the additional belittling of the student body. Those moments were darkly enraging, deeply isolating. These reactions of my peer group ultimately provided more fuel to the fire, encouraging my further disruption, regardless of the insinuations of folly that came my way. I felt disdain for these characters co-operating in their own oppression. It was paramount I keep them at some distance. They represented what I could become if I wasn't careful - scared, weak, cowardly, non-creative, without virtue.

Application form in hand, I at least recognised the significance of what I was about to commit to writing. The problem was I knew nothing of an alternative, had no better suggestions. School did not prepare me for this moment. I felt devoid of the tools required to make informed decisions.

Even if I had chosen to be an attentive and earnest student, it would have made no difference. There was nothing formally offered during my previous 12 years of education that contributed to my ability to understand anything I felt to be important. I had been fed information for over a decade, little of which appeared relevant to a fulfilling life. Nothing offered provided inspiration, nothing appeared to facilitate a moving out into the world in a way that would aid development as an effective contributor to a virtuous society. Rather, the information had the opposite effect, it was confusing to my awareness of who I was, and the worldly context within which this has meaning. Surely, in order to make a choice, it is best first to know as much as possible regarding the 'who' for which the choice is being made. I could not remember significant instances of encouragement towards a self-familiarity. It was rare to be asked of my preferences, even for dinner. I can't recall a time when anyone enquired sincerely after my well-being. Was the question, "How are you?" ever meant to be taken literally?

I chose Law. I chose Law because my brother, older by one year, was already a student in the faculty. I chose it because of the 100% confidence I had in this decision being well met by my parent's approval. I chose it because I knew of no other preferable choices. I chose it because this would allow me to give choosing a break. Hindsight suggests I was in no position to choose.

Those that would become my fellow students were not convincing me of their passion for their chosen path either. They appeared more like they were continuing on the path of following orders, wearing the straitjacket, still behaving themselves. What a polite, insincere, untrustworthy, misguided bunch they appeared. The probability these guys were as clueless as I in what course of action to take was of no comfort.

re-membering

There was of course societal kudos connected with acceptance into such schools, as there was for other elite schools such as medicine, dentistry, engineering or architecture. The fact lawyers often attracted substantial influence and money was not lost on many of my fellow undergraduates. Though not a word was mentioned in admiration for the legal system, nothing about ways through which its integrity could be improved. On the contrary, general references to the system were in jest. Sarcasm and cynicism constituted the currency of conversation.

My new peers were motivated by competition. This became more clearly apparent during periods of assessment. At such times, all relevant reference books would disappear from the library and even students with whom I was most acquainted gave vague, unhelpful responses when questioned regarding the content of such assessments. Admittedly, my inquiries were only necessary because of my serial absence from formal course lectures in the first place.

∞

My period of enrolment was spent mainly in honing my skills at computer games and pinball machines. My pinball credentials had been developing since early adolescence. During that period I would forego eating lunch in order to use my allowance to buy potato scallops and fund my ritual pinball sessions on my way home from school. In this way I was able to disappear through the cracks of my surveilled childhood.

I developed my abilities to the point only a single coin was required to start me off, as I would then continue on the basis of winning free replays. My enthusiasm for this pastime dimmed in my later adolescence when game arcades began to increase the tilt factor on my favoured machines. A tilt, and the resulting suspension of play, occurs when the machine is bumped over a threshold force. However, such force is required in order to maximise control of the ball, essential if a player is to exercise sufficient mastery to win further games. This stacked the odds against me to the point of undermining my success.

Of course this lifestyle produced dismal academic results. In my first year I failed everything I bothered to sit for. My father was so angry he went as far as to accuse my friends of being a bad influence on me. A cowardly move on his part, I felt. Although perhaps this diverted his wrath away from blaming me and thus away from the possibility of losing control and doing serious damage to my physique.

∞

During the era that framed my early post-school years, Australians were enjoying an unprecedented degree of financial prosperity. The welfare system was handing out generous amounts of cash. The unemployed were paid an allowance in return for listing two jobs they may or may not have applied for over the last fortnight. For those willing to work, there was plenty on offer with good pay and conditions. University courses were free, and money was provided to students to cover living costs. Interestingly, the economic climate of prosperity coincided with my personal discontent. Would it have been better to have been limited for choice? Does a lack of choice lead to a calming of confusion, a bringing of focus, a relief from concern? In my case I very much doubt it.

∞

I left Law at the end of my first year and quickly landed a job in the local council. With my appointment I was provided flexible working hours within a 36-hour working week. I was immediately provided a generous income, a socially stimulating inner city work place location, and all the while, responsibilities of no great challenge. On the top floor of the council building was a club designed for the benefit of the council's many employees. It provided subsidised meals and alcohol, with entertainment on some nights, especially on Friday.

I began my white-collar life on the 10th of the 21 floors. Mark, my former classmate and friend now of some years, had already taken up employment on the 4th floor. As if things could get even better, I was soon posted downstairs on the mezzanine floor. Here the public could gain access to any of the council's various departments and services through representatives. Personally, I not only represented my Works Department office, but also Health and Parks.

As the sole representative of these departments I sat unsupervised. Law firms provided my most regular of clients in the shape of the sexy young secretaries who conveyed written requests for property data. Mark and I regularly met at the club for liquid lunches which often overflowed the maximum permissible two-hour lunch break. The quantity of alcohol consumed had the effect of dragging out the afternoon shift, encouraging regular early finishes at 4pm, more or less.

This personal responsibility was a novelty, one for which I cared little. I was not always attentive to delivering the minimal services of which I was required. Curiously it was not the drinking that was my downfall. It was the suggestion of a ratepayer that I had promised for a council truck to come and pick up unwanted materials from his footpath that became the pretext for my decline. This disgruntled citizen proceeded to contact my boss when the service was not forth-coming. My boss felt pressured to do something about it. I was accused of promising a service the council did not offer, this without ever being asked of what really happened. To this day I can't remember if I actually did that of which I was accused.

It didn't matter. I soon found myself transferred out of my former comfortable position, and into a works depot where I was to take up the position of salaries clerk. Among employees it was a commonly held belief that no-one gets fired from the council. Certainly there was some evidence of this from within my own department. A member of my former office had the responsibility of handling fortnightly wage payments, at the time being cash. This guy attempted to do a runner with the payload, only to be caught at the airport and feature on that night's TV news. Even he was not sacked. He was transferred to a works depot.

My new office was drab and grey. Nobody was there due to heart's desire. No-one there was even enjoying some kind of stimulating experience. The atmosphere was bleak. I arrived to work early in the mornings in order to be there before the boss and fudge my starting time, aiding an early exit. I was eventually caught for this indiscretion.

I began to plan my exit. I considered giving Law another go, but this time a sincere attempt. The main motivation for this, in retrospect vainly flawed, was to prove to myself I could do it. This is what I did. Although my results were better, no failures, they were still not outstanding. My heart was not in it despite my efforts. I ended up in tears on the university lawn. Still I was without a lead on what I should do with my life.

∞

In the absence of any better ideas, I returned to white collar work, this time as a salaries clerk at Queensland University. At the interview, the section and department boss asked if I was looking at sinking my roots.

Obviously they were angling for someone who would stay the distance, and thus contribute to a stable staff line-up. I told them what they wanted to hear, and they gave me the nod.

On the bus out of the university campus one afternoon, on expressing my doubt of longevity within the post, one of my fellow female employees mentioned not to be concerned as after 10 years of work, 13 weeks of paid long service leave would become available. The scenario was deeply depressing. This was the start of an affliction that hung over me for almost a complete calendar year.

There is no clear consensus within the medical profession on the best treatment for depression. Reportedly its causes are manifold. Negative personal life events, family history, personality, serious illness, drug and alcohol abuse have all been linked. What is most concerning is that a medication that modifies brain chemistry may be considered a successful treatment due to its ability to temporarily relieve and replace undesirable symptoms with feelings of well-being, a state that would otherwise naturally arise through the execution of one's life in alignment with the most heartfelt of personal motivations.

Was industrialised society failing to provide a sufficient foundation for a fulfilling life for many, and then medicating relief from this message within its more perturbed individuals? Specifically, in the workplace were drugs effectively hijacking a natural signal arising as a reaction to the meaningless repetition of mundane occupation? How much time had medical researchers in this field spent in sincere consideration of the repercussions of their recommendations? Of course medication could only continue as a response if their remained a blurring of any direct and causal connection between occupation and ill-health.

In my case I did not doubt that my depression was directly connected to a lack of engagement in anything meaningful. How I felt was clearly not born of a lack of opportunity to engage in all that my native culture and its offshoot counter-culture offered. Though a job for its own sake was not enough of a reason for the job, financial security didn't motivate me, studying to be a professional didn't impassion me, friends and girlfriend offered insufficient relief, and counter-culture, well, lots of words, but no workable foundation for a sustainable life.

Every day I would be weighed down by the heaviness of depression from the early moments of waking, and within that state I would remain till I fell to sleep at night. There was no one I trusted sufficiently with which to talk about it. I felt that those who surrounded me were either likely to taunt me for my display of weakness, become negatively affected by taking my revelations personally, or become fearful of what I might do next and the responsibility that made them feel.

I withdrew. I isolated myself by increasing degrees. My girlfriend was one of my last companions standing. I ultimately wanted to break up with her as well, but her graspy opposition to any such idea tended to discourage me from adding further drama and difficulty to my life. Of course there were repercussions. Resentment arrived. I told her I hated her and had an affair. These passive aggressions still did not dissuade her. These actions and omissions were obviously not helping. Rather they were paving a downward path to some dark and destructive conclusion.

Meanwhile the depression did not feel out of place. In fact it may have been the perfect resulting predicament to my dilemma. It sat me on my arse and it wasn't going to let me out of its grip until a solution was found. No distraction would do. No pleasure would do.

At night I sat and watched the television. I had been watching a documentary series on Chinese culture. It appeared so exotic, so different, so appealing. At the time the country was closed to visitors, but the programme awoke something in me. In retrospect, I might say this country appeared so different that it stimulated attraction as a place that may contain something for me, something unavailable within my own culture. I resolved to save money and take a trip, a trip at least to the general region of Asia.

I doubled and re-doubled my efforts to save as fast as I could. I took a second job, at night, working at a bottlo - a drive through alcohol shop. I started selling weed again. In the latter, I was ripped off through my naïve dealings with untrustworthy middlemen. The value of the Australian dollar decreased dramatically due to a floating of the currency by the federal government, leading to a rapid 30% reduction in the value of my money overseas. Regardless, nothing would get in my way. There was no time to lose.

the trail of scattered breadcrumbs

My uncle maintained an expression of condescension as he looked me up and down at the airport departure. I reacted with proud defiance, feeling vindicated in my appearance. Though in retrospect I could empathise with his point of view. My oversized second-hand jumper was far from anything he would have chosen to wear in public. The quality of my clothing was not at all dissimilar to that of the men who routinely bedded down in the local park. My uncle's generation had devoted their life to toil towards an existence more materially prosperous than that of their parents, that of their own childhood. Within this devotion laid a significant portion of their pride.

Farewells were hurriedly exchanged with the uncomfortable, dissociative emotional restraint characteristic of that cultural period. In the awkward space that ensued these formalities my front crumbled, giving way to a palpable sense of aloneness. This feeling had been a regular companion for a while now, and so it was as I turned and wandered away from the final vestiges of my youth.

re-membering

This was my first instance of feeling devoid of a physical community. The experience of society's major institutions had, piece by piece, fragment by fragment dissolved the attachments that had previously provided a low-resolution confusion of meanings known to most as a normal life. This resulted in isolation, and further increased my yearnings for succour. But my sense of well-being required more than normal. This message was being communicated through my deepest of known resonances. It was these that impassioned my earlier rebellion, and, in turn, led to my present casting away.

As might a lost lamb, I joined the first queue I came across. Upon inquiring of a pair of Swedish backpackers standing directly ahead, it was revealed I was standing with a group bound for Europe. I gleaned enough from the interaction to inform of where I might search further for my place of departure. Course corrected, I managed to find my line and flight. Seated within my allocation, I found easy company in an Irishman opposite, and with this, all immediate qualms dissolved.

The six-hour trip allowed for early friendly banter to develop into a dialogue regarding what mattered to each of us. Tom, similar to all of the few Irish men I had met, provided a proud, witty disposition, with a passion for domestic affairs. Being of Irish ancestry, I was already aware of the tensions in the north of his island home between the Protestants and the Catholics. I knew of the notorious Irish Republican Army (IRA). Tom informed me of further detail, of the existence of the political Sinn Fein and their goal in common with the IRA to unify the island as a single country. He detailed his personal involvement, and in doing so portrayed perspectives that formed much of what life meant to him.

I became fleetingly envious of my new companion. He had a community and they were united by a common cause. The cause related to place, to what defined home, one of the deepest of identifications. It was not my battle, though I got a taste for the fight worth fighting. I reassured myself that my goal lay elsewhere. I had a home, or at least, had had a home. It had been my choice to walk away.

Upon touching down in Bali, I was met at immigration by an intimidating figure in uniform. I was struck by a sense that, for this man, extinguishing my life would not be of great concern. His intense stare was unsettling. Perhaps it was part of a conscious ploy to undermine the guise of an arrival who was concealing what was his duty to reveal. Maybe my appearance prompted a common association with illegal substances. Indonesian drug laws are strict, and depending on quantity, a death sentence often awaits conviction for importation. A degree of tension quickly spread through my body, although this was tempered by the knowledge that I did not possess any such substance. On the other hand, regardless of innocence, outcomes are not always assured by the facts. Uncertainty, doubt, paranoia, panic, how far was I willing to let myself go? Of course it was impossible to know what, if anything, passed through the mind of this officer, or what sort of a day or a life he was having. He eventually thrust a visa and stamp into the first page of my passport, passing it back into my possession and releasing me with a turn of his head.

Tom and I shared a taxi in to Kuta Beach. This is the most common of all visitor destinations on the island and only a few kilometres from the airport. The taxi was a Holden sedan. This iconic Australian vehicle of the era provided early evidence of this region's inter-connectedness. A seemingly unperturbed Tom sat opposite in the back seat, providing comfort to my total lack of experience.

Outside the rolled-down window, the streets appeared dirty and strewn with litter. The air rushing my nostrils contained a complex mix of odours, combining in a cocktail not dissimilar to sewage, no doubt enhanced by the fermenting effects of the tropical heat. The stimuli flooding my senses combined to an effect primarily welcomed. The scene stood in contrast to the prior ordered, familiar, constricting habitat that for so long had correlated with my personal feelings of emptiness. I now quietly celebrated its consignment to the past.

Upon arrival in Kuta, we left the vehicle and proceeded on foot. Accommodation was plentiful and so convenient for comparison. All viewed options existed within walled perimeters, the interior compound generally laid out with guest rooms to the rear and family residence closer to the entrance. Chickens commonly ranged freely. As it was already late in the day, we settled on a place without much deliberation. The concrete boxes constructed to house guests were less than ideal, but the front veranda all rooms shared provided a pleasant place to sit and view the garden, and a place to watch the family as they went about their lives.

Our neighbours were a pair of Australian surfers. Their presence further reinforced my understanding I had left my country but still remained close. These guys were chilled. Their dispositions reflected the power of the ocean in moulding those that submerge within her immensity as a way of life. Our new acquaintances looked at home here. Unsurprisingly, this was not their first visit. At the time of our arrival, they were organising for departure on their night's activities. During their preparations they occasionally detoured in order to share a joint of their own supply.

I quickly found myself delivered into an intense awareness of my surroundings. The unfamiliar now became highlighted. The environment now struck me as starkly alien. I instinctively scanned for any signs of threat, and then began to attend to more detail. As I was unpractised in the art of sincere emotional expression, I remained silent as to my state of mind. In due course, the surfers disappeared into the evening. Tom retired to inside our shared concrete box. I had been left alone, seated upon the front stair. The Sun set. Dusk was upon me.

The garden area was still sufficiently lit to make out its contents. The presence of the children playing in the fading light and the occasional chicken scurrying for safety brought some peace of mind, though my body was still on full alert. A boy of around 10 years arrived carrying a mosquito coil. He proceeded to light and place the coil on an empty beer bottle to one side of the entrance of our room. I managed a half-smile, caught between my appreciation for the offering of the child, and my inability to come to terms with my new environment.

I fell to pondering the importance of bolstering my confidence in order to make the most of this chance. There was meaning in terming this outing as a rite of passage. My life's fulfilment felt dependent upon the good use of this opportunity. It was going to take some time to develop the necessary courage. At least time was something of which I felt I had sufficient. I was 22 years old and had funds to get started. I wasn't sure where I was going. This lack of certainty regarding my future did not bother me overly as I was keenly aware of what awaits at the end of it all. Whatever was to become of this trip could not exceed this in its import. First and foremost I needed to find my travel legs. This conclusion segued sharply back into a now quiet and still presence...

In comparison to the dirty and littered streets, this domestic courtyard is an impressive sanctuary. Beauty emanates from the life that inhabits its living space. It is well-kept, with an abundance of plants and trees. The entrance is guarded by a spirit house, spirits within their own abode. It feels as a safe space for family life, to which the home is central. The abode is clearly not just a place to rest. It is much more. It is where many of life's key events take place...

"Are you hungry?"

Tom's already familiar accented voice arrived from the interior of our room. In this situation even the fulfilling of this most fundamental of life's needs felt a worthy challenge. The presence of my first travel companion again allowed for easier organisation and execution of such essential activities. I managed to convey sufficient interest in eating to co-operate a decision. Tom's tall frame emerged from the shadows of the room. This prompted my wallet-retrieval and pack-stowing. After I exited the room, Tom proceeded to lock the door. Following his lead, we moved out of the compound and into the laneway. The path formed part of a lattice. Becoming lost appeared to be the easiest of potential outcomes.

Conveniently we quickly came upon a restaurant. It was softly lit though stood out against the darkness that shrouded the sand upon which we found our way. It was a hut no larger than a standard living room. Immediately appealing was its construction, the entrance through a side with no wall present. The three existing walls appeared to be of thatched bamboo. A simple and economical design to great effect, it presented guests with unobscured exterior views of palms and shrubs, illuminated from inside by the candles placed upon each dining table.

We were immediately greeted with a relaxed smile and a pair of lustrous eyes, set within the smooth brown face of our host. I had never before witnessed such a combination of beauty, serenity, grace, attentiveness. These traits felt as of a single benevolent source. The effect was immediately disarming. It substantially appeased my prior unease.

My lack of familiarity with local food and my drive to acquaint myself with the details of this exotic culture resulted in considerable time spent pouring over the menu. Tom did not share my level of curiosity. He had been through this part of the world previously. In fact he was on his way back home, Australia having been the southernmost extent of his itinerary. It was his travel stories that now occupied most of what was shared between us. I was especially interested in how to go about arranging all required to enable novel experience while at the same time remaining safe, economical, and comfortable. The more intelligence I gathered however, the less interested I became. Logistics beyond the details of my next move were looking increasingly like unnecessary distraction.

My first course arrived, half of a beautifully ripe avocado. The space opened up by the fruit's deseeding had been half-filled with a garlic-infused vegetable oil. The flesh stood in cross-section, revealed in its various shades of green through yellow. This simple offering received within this structure of natural materials, served with attentive, warm service, engendered further restfulness and a deepening sense of well-being.

I was quickly gaining assurance in my undertaking. Early evidence hinted that this adventure may be enjoyed with less concern, even solo. I was not really alone anyway. I was surrounded by people, people revealing as not all out to get me, people going about their lives not merely driven by profit at my expense. My earliest impressions were of a local community animated by an inner sense of being part of something much larger than themselves.

∞

Over the following days I explored all that engaged my curiosity. The island is famous for its beaches, though this natural beauty represented an environment significant within my past, and I was in search of the new. The many cultural artifacts on display formed an alluring part of the visual landscape. Paintings, rock and wood carvings, silverware, all spoke loudly of the primacy of the aesthetic within the mind of the native inhabitants.

I quickly found many of my fellow travellers displayed no more than a cursory interest in such things, and more generally, in the way the place and people may inform of new perspectives on lifestyle. Commonly visitors appeared to more value socialising among themselves in the manner of their homeland, making use of the surrounds for the purpose of an exotic backdrop for relaxation. I found myself increasingly in avoidance of such company.

Tom moved on before me. I moved to an oceanside bungalow. After taking a few days to acclimatise myself to managing alone, I moved away from the coast, up through the centre of the island. I attempted a visit to a volcano, though was prohibited entry by a pack of feral dogs that insisted on my full respect. My experience of the north was significantly enhanced and extended through pleasant female company, girls exhibiting traits that their travels had probably nurtured and amplified, an open-mindedness and an ability to listen as much as to express themselves.

Moving from the small population of Hindus on the small island of Bali to the huge population of Muslims on the larger island of Java is a transition perhaps lost on no traveller. Though hospitable, there appeared little of personal interest amid much to negotiate. It was in Yogyakarta, a place in which I took a break from the at times hectic experience of moving around, where I met the news China was open to visitors. This filled me with excitement, there being my first inspiration for travel. My decision was made clear. I immediately set about researching how I would plot my path.

∞

re-membering

To attempt to describe Chungking Mansions in a few words is to deprive it of so much impressive detail. Its seventeen floors encase volumes. Exteriorly derelict among its modern neighbours, interiorly foreboding through its exposed wiring, intermittent stairwell water cascades, narrow corridors and dim recesses, the place provides an extraordinary backdrop against which passing actors live out their respective dramas.

It's a vast and diverse cast of the impromptu, with plots and sub-plots consistently circling around the end that is cash, by many means. Above the planned business dealings of ground floor retail, inhabitants had improvised eateries and accommodations within rooms originally intended for long term domestic apartment living. Over time the Mansions had been cased and deemed suitable as a hideaway for prostitution services, its halls as rendezvous for drug dealings. It became notorious as a centre for smuggling and a base for underworld operations. These intricate internal workings placed pressure on the systems and networks that maintained its ecology. Electrical fires and assaults were not uncommon and at times had proven fatal.

Amid the unprecedented level of turmoil that is Kowloon's street life, within the limits of time, energy and money I was willing to expend, alternatives to the Mansions as a place to stay appeared in short supply. I purposefully chose a room no higher than the sixth floor so as to be able to exit quickly down the stairs in the event of a lift malfunction, or due to some other unforeseen emergency.

I had found my way to Hong Kong in reasonably direct fashion. At first, mysterious symptoms briefly waylaid plans in Singapore. It started with chills and fever and ended the following morning in a pool of sweat, though in full recovery. The night previous, sitting alone on a bunk within that small dormitory, repeatedly draping and then releasing the hostel-supplied blanket from around me, I had not been confident of whether I was to see it through.

An easy hitchhiking experience followed, transporting me over the Malaysian Peninsula and leaving me grateful to the youthful Malay in a sports car, the Chinese couple in a Volvo, and the Indian at the wheel of a semi-trailer who together played my hosts. The combined show of generosity from across the country's main racial and religious groups displayed a common generosity amid racial diversity. My experience was thus positive, though this modern and organised part of the world developed through the mutual effort of these same ethnicities reflected an interest in material gain I had already left behind. From the country's northern border I sat a train journey to Bangkok, from where I arranged a same day flight out in a desire to detour the troubling inconvenience presented by that large, polluted city.

On my first night in Hong Kong I ate dinner within the Mansions, in the lounge room of an Indian family. They hadn't bothered to create much of a pretence of a commercial enterprise, simply a sign conspicuously placed in the outside hallway and menus on the single interior table. I sat and watched television with the children while I ate.

After dinner I took the journey downstairs and out into the early evening. The streets provided greater space, more light, fresh air, and eventually company. The night had thinned pedestrians to a comfortable density. This made it possible to make out more detail among and within the passers-by.

Tomas had also just finished dinner and was out orienting himself to his new surrounds. Our initial point of contact was seamlessly negotiated, and developed in the same manner. I was excited to happen across someone with whom I quickly found seemingly anything could be discussed. After it became clear there was more to be gained from furthering the conversation, Tomas suggested we retire to more comfortable surrounds. He had an idea for a suitable location and so led the way to a nearby upmarket hotel and in through its automatic sliding doors. We made our way to an area with luxurious seating that made up one corner of the ground floor at a comfortable distance from reception. Here we would be left alone.

Tomas was from Sweden. His country was in a part of the world about which I was most curious. My uninformed perspective was one of an open-minded, intelligent population within a small and beautiful country.

He mentioned he had been to Australia and I enquired about his impressions. After some time seemingly in search of the right words, he answered, "There is no debate." I was astonished by his resonant reply. He had summarised a significant factor that had contributed to my prior sense of aloneness and ultimately to my desperation to leave. His pronouncement further encouraged within me a will to share and explore ideas and perspectives I had formerly found little grounds for expression. We continued our conversation late into the night. It was only when fatigue began to descend that we agreed to go our separate ways.

Days passed with minimal forward movement on my part. I hadn't planned to be here for more than the time required to prepare to cross into the mainland, although a few days soon became a week, and then two. I changed my place of stay, to a comparatively short building, one of six floors where the roof provided seating, cooking facilities and a bathroom.

This rooftop was a gathering place for the building's temporary guests, and where I spent much of my time. My planned move into China felt somewhat daunting, and while I was able to gather a little more first-hand intelligence from the few travellers I met who had just left the country, I was essentially hesitating. My rooftop company had become a comfortable distraction. However, the departure day did finally arrive.

∞

It was easy to believe the population of the whole country exceeded one billion upon arriving in Guangzhou. I felt it in the frenzy that greeted me upon exiting the train. I was shocked, culturally, again, though this time without the aid of a mind-enhancing ally. The very atmosphere was mind-enhancing. Again my mind was brought to sharp focus, sharp and broad at the same time. Confusion scanned for detail without knowing where specifically to look.

The hive-like out bursting did not let up. There was nowhere to hide. The sheer number of humans contributed to a staggering competition for resources of all descriptions, space on sidewalks, seats in restaurants, places in queues, audibility through which to be heard, all activity conducted with an absence of ceremony. Lines of customers leaked and burst into wedges, restaurant floors accumulated bones and phlegm to be hosed out at the end of the night. The very language of the natives appeared strikingly well-evolved to cut through the din.

I remained on the move in search of some air to breathe, some space to privately occupy, somewhere that was not just people. It was as tiring as it was fascinating. The more I moved, the more I was exposed to the chaotic order. The sheer weight of numbers created a sense of being personally unimportant, individually insignificant. Situations consistently challenged me to throw off my conditioning and remould my faltering humanity in order to achieve the most basic of tasks. It challenged me to behave in a manner considered rude, at times inhumane, from the perspective of my native culture. There was no time for strangers, no place for kindness. This was an exposure to another shade of what I could be, comparatively more different than similar to that which with I had previously negotiated.

There were other places. There was nature. There was beauty. Though I did not settle until I also found a sufficient sense of community, as much as can be expected while on the move. My criteria directed me across the south of the country. Here the weather remained comparatively warm as year's end approached. I chose Kunming as a base, a large provincial capital, though one central to a variety of attractive destinations to the south and west.

It was true China had recently opened to foreign tourists, but this came with conditions and limitations. Only specific places were welcome to foreigners, and for most of these an extra permit was required. It was explained that due to reasons of military conflict, a lack of suitable infrastructure, or extreme poverty, many places were deemed unsuitable for foreign visitation.

I managed to locate a large hotel designated to receive overseas guests. Moving to reception, I glanced at the two females who sat on the other side of the counter. They were dressed in the standard green uniform and bobbed hair of the era. It was as if appearances were fashioned to as much as possible eliminate difference, between and within gender. Whatever the reason, regulation strove vainly in a direction opposite to that which accentuates the beautiful, opposite to the natural order of things.

I waited for service. Local guests came, shouted their needs, and when obliged, disappeared without a smile or a word of gratitude. It became clear if I didn't assert myself, I would not be attended. No English was spoken. I resorted to exaggerated theatre, creatively expressing my request through mime.

I was led up a concrete staircase and down a hall to a large dormitory that accommodated only non-Chinese persons. It was clear from the presence of backpacks the room was about half occupied. Most of the luggage owners were not present. My neighbours were busily attending to their huge packs and their various forms of photographic equipment. They were obviously preparing for their imminent departure.

My fellow travellers' mindset was mirrored through the amount of their accompanying possessions and careful concern for their safe keeping. They had brought as much of home with them as they could carry, and thus would have to spend a significant amount of time attending to these items. The photographic equipment suggested the trip was preoccupied with developing a narrative, something with which to impress others, or perhaps their future selves. All this at the expense of novel experience, I thought.

I too had brought a camera, a gift from my now ex-girlfriend. I too had made it a priority to take good photos. This was not that easy. It ate up a lot of my time. It was also influencing my decisions. It was drawing my attention. It had become a distraction. I felt that it was inhibiting the spontaneity required to further other potential opportunities. I ended up giving the memory machine away. This immediately simplified my decision making, and most importantly opened me up more to the world going on around me.

After setting down my pack, I gathered my passport and money and exited the hotel. I followed the road in the direction best illuminated, and thus, I guessed, of the most human activity. After eating surprisingly tasty, inexpensive food in the relaxed atmosphere of a side street vegetarian restaurant, I continued wandering and wondering. I passed landscaped gardens that punctuated the wide sidewalk. To my surprise one of these gardens housed a familiar type of tree that stood taller than my height. On closer inspection I realised it was indeed a marijuana plant. It had obviously been intended as a feature due to its central place and dominant form. The plant was budding.

I surveyed my surroundings to confirm I was not being observed. At this time of night, in this non-residential part of town, with shop fronts closed, there were no other pedestrians in sight. As far as I could see, I was alone. I singled out a medium size branch in an area of the tree comparatively thick with growth. Careful as to not compromise the plants aesthetic value, I worked the branch close to the main trunk, up and down, twist, repeat. Using the fingers of my left hand I was able to limit the impact to the local area, pinching against the bark to avoid tearing down the trunk. I managed to sever the branch without much damage to the plant. I slid the branch up the inside of my winter jacket and so smuggled my harvest back to the hotel.

In the morning I awoke to the sound of unrestrained throat-clearing coming from outside the room. This behaviour was clearly sanctioned due to the placement of spittoons at regular intervals along the hotel corridors. Most of the travellers with which I shared space had already gone out. I appreciated this as it meant I could start my day amid quiet. I began with basic language study with the aid of my travel guide. This ceased when my focus began to fade and hunger began to draw my attention.

I retrieved the marijuana branch from under my bunk and laid it out to dry on the roof that sheltered the hallway. The buds on the branch appeared to be of reasonable quality for consumption despite the plant not being raised for its psychoactive properties. The buds were small, though dense, with an aroma that suggested a considerable oil content. I shared the story of my find with a few foreign travellers who were sharing my dorm.

That evening as I again passed the landscaped garden, I had a rude awakening. The whole plant had been stripped bare. In a single blow, the site of this devastation completely disillusioned me of the idea travellers held a common ethos of low-impact, of taking care, of leaving things as they were found. From then I became further discerning of my company, and to whom I said what. This had a summarly positive effect. I became more focused on what really mattered for me to achieve, more efficient, and less socially needy.

∞

Marijuana continued to show up in my path. Within the beautiful surrounds of Dali, a few 100 kilometres to the west of the capital, the plant grew in dispersed stands, within the walled enclosures of residential yards and in the wild. The local's only use for the plant was stated as limited to the burning of its seeds as incense at temples. After harvesting some branches and laying them out at a local café I frequented, the owners asked me what use I had for it. With perhaps misplaced concern, I hedged that it was good for digestion.

Dali sits on the shore of a 40 km long lake within the view of an impressive snow-capped mountain range that runs parallel to the long shoreline. This village remained a consistently comfortable base from which to go off on adventures, situated in a part of the country that accessed the borderlands to the south and the foothills of the Himalayas to the north-west.

re-membering

Of course, the region should become extremely cold with altitude. Although at the time there existed scant available information that could serve to verify this or any other prevailing conditions of travel. There was no accessible English language news. The occasional word-of-mouth story that fed back and forth among foreign travellers along prohibited routes of passage was all, and that source of the nature of anecdote, almost mythical in its quality.

During my months there I heard various stories of travellers suffering hyperthermia to the point of their demise while hitchhiking through the snow-covered mountains that lined the long, long shortcut to Tibet. These stories effectively warned of an element of non-negotiable limitation to adventure in this part of the world. They also highlighted an element of pragmatism within the country's regulation of foreigner's travel destinations.

I was pleasantly surprised and impressed here by the common presence of Scandinavians, especially females travelling alone. It was summer holiday time in those countries and China could be accessed from the north via the trans-Siberian railway. At the time I considered the girls from that region of incomparable beauty. I had already met Swedes and Norwegians on my way to and while staying in Dali, but it was a Danish girl with whom I planned my first trip towards the forbidden areas directly north.

I had already grown somewhat accustomed to the attention I was getting from the public, being a foreigner in a region that had only recently been exposed to my type, but to set off on a journey to places where foreigners were forbidden in the company of a tall, pale, blonde, blue-eyed female was to present the greatest of contrasts to and for the local inhabitants.

Once we were out of foreigner-approved Dali the conditions became more extreme by all measures. Beyond the expected changes in altitude and temperature, buses overcrowded to the point of people attempting to climb in through the windows and clamber on to the roof as the driver went after them with a stick. Naked poverty increasingly startled my eyes in townships the further we proceeded. As our presence gained greater attention, I suggested Daniela cover her head with a scarf. The folly of this response was not lost on me, though I still felt the need to try and do something.

When we stepped down from the bus at its final stop, we quickly drew a crowd of around 100 people. The locals stared in a way that displayed no acknowledgement of common humanity. It felt akin to being an alien. Feeling beyond uncomfortable, patience disappeared, and anger arose. I unleashed in voice and waved arms in a shooing motion. This drew even greater curiosity. The onlooker's smiles of incredulity broadened, exchanged commentary increased, stares intensified as if in anticipation of my continuing anomalous display.

The crowd continued to rapidly coalesce and intensify. Desperation turned me to Daniela. Grabbing her arm, I led her at speed down a side street and into a hotel. The younger crowd members quickly set out in chase. We ran down a hallway and sought temporary refuge in a bathroom. We shut the door, on the inside of which I placed an ear. Some of the children had found their way down the corridor and were now milling and chattering outside. I felt we needed to simply wait this one out. After a short while they retreated.

This region is home for a great diversity of ethnic groups. On an early outing we came across a man dressed from head cap to shoes in white, mounted upon a white horse. The garb rendered him almost invisible against the snow-covered terrain that surrounded the town. From the quality of his well-fitting clothing through to his upright posture and spirited steed, the total presence stimulated my imagination toward some far away time and place. I could only guess that his ancestors had arrived in the area via the Silk Road sometime in the distant past.

In contrasting uniform black, a troupe of women carrying large bundles of wood upon their shoulders was next to catch our attention. We followed these women on a trek over some hills and down into a small village. Upon exploring the settlement's few streets, we came across and entered a temple.

Here, as at many of the rural temples, graffiti had been scrawled, large pictographs in red paint stood out against the background of the white-washed walls. The stark renderings were obviously there to promote a damning message. Buddhism was not spared the general accusation of inextricable connection with the exploitative classes. The destruction of such institutions was held to be an essential part of cleansing the minds of the populous from the poison that had held them down for so long. The graffiti was not only evidence of the passing presence of Mao's red guards during the Cultural Revolution at least 10 years earlier, but also that such revolutionary authority still loomed threateningly.

Inside the temple a hospitable old man enthusiastically invited us for tea. Not dressed in the way of a monk, perhaps not allowed to, he appeared to be engaged with basic caretaking responsibilities. We proceeded in a long communication without the aid of a common language. Suffice to say explanations relied significantly upon dramatisation. Driven by mutual will, we were able to interact regarding various subjects including details of the destruction at the hands of the red guards. It was obviously still fresh in the guy's memory.

The old man did not diminish in his animated descriptions as our interaction continued and the daylight began to fade. He ignited a fire within the confines of a large drum, interspersing the addition of dried branches with continued passionate story-telling. After the flames and exchange began to dwindle, he extended an offer of a place to rest. I had been so immersed within the interaction that I remained reluctant to consider the dark, cold distance of the unfamiliar territory now separating us from our hotel room. The experience to that point had been so wonderful that to digress felt as to turn away from what was so important to appreciate. My heart was alive to the adventure. I had also met no resistance from within my company. Daniela, although young and inexperienced, remained in trust of the situation. Suffice to say, we spent the night.

∞

Of course, this sojourn through the rural regions did not always deliver such conviviality. What it did deliver consistently however were experiences that fed my desire for knowledge. To this end, opportunities were arising through a willingness to engage with new challenges at many levels. Meaning was revealing itself through experiences that served to expose and encourage the shedding of accumulated limiting beliefs. That which had been previously insisted upon as barriers were now showing up as invitations to creative negotiation. There was continuing unexpected richness in challenging the nominally prohibited. There was immeasurable value in communicating with those who spoke of a different time, place, and circumstance. Race, culture, religion, language, all were now conceptually repositioning themselves. They were not there to be judged. They were sets of ideas which presented tools with which to explore and contrast differing world views. Characters were being revealed alive with a nature beyond easy characterisation. Personally, the experience was inspiring a burgeoning where-with-all, an emerging capability and flexibility beyond which I had previously known as possible.

∞

I recall my brief romancing of itinerary-creation back in Bali. I remember quickly resigning to the much greater efficiency of a mere pre-determined destination of personal relevance and the most interesting line that joined there with here. The line was now drawn through Kunming – Tibet – Nepal – India. I had ruminated on the possibility of taking the direct route to Tibet, though those stories of prior traveller deaths had given me pause. The alternative was the circuitous route, the more than 2 000 km journey to the north, before doubling back on a merciless seat atop crude shock absorption over long stretches of corrugated dirt road.

Before the time that decision became relevant it was no longer available. I heard from a number of travellers certain mountain passes between Tibet and Nepal had been rendered unpassable by heavy snow fall, indefinitely. I had delayed any earlier onward movement since consenting to a rendezvous with my ex-girlfriend who was now on her way over for a short visit. This necessitated a return to Kunming where we had arranged to meet up.

After a short allowance for acclimatisation for Linda, and rest and nutrition for myself, we set off on a route more directly north. In the afternoon we arrived into a large industrial town. Grey factories belched grey smoke into grey skies. Grey water flowed under the grey metal bridge our bus traversed on its way to the city centre. Through prolonged absence of the familiar, my interpretations of the surrounds were now loosening, further unleashing the imagination. The scene felt as of a more archetypal nature, drawing more towards something of a dreamscape. The real was dissolving to the surreal, more overwhelmingly intrusive, less dependable.

All other passengers stood up and pushed towards the doors as we pulled into a large station. The driver killed the engine. Our transport had terminated. After stepping down we began our search for a place to stay. If there were any taxis, they were not forthcoming nor in any way conspicuous.

In fact my entire experience of the country's larger urban centres remained starkly absent of persons attempting to engage me in any type of business transaction. In the now four months since my arrival I saw none of it. One Guangzhou bank employee of fleeting acquaintance confided that the central government instructed citizens to maintain a friendly face, though not engage with the foreign ghosts (鬼佬). This was certainly consistent with my experience of the places dominated by the majority Han Chinese. It had been a different story in the rural areas among the communities of racial minorities.

I continued to absorb the atmosphere as we walked. The impersonal nature of the experience made for a relative ease of vicarious enjoyment. Within the pressing confines of surrounding concrete and the swirl of trapped vehicle emissions there still remained an intense ethereal quality. The singular presence of solely human-made forms sustained a brutal assault. Though weirdly enchanting, I felt no compulsion to dwell. There was nothing endearing about this place. Further, such large population centres necessitate increased law and order, and harbour the authority to enforce it. If not for the lateness of the day and the idea of a welcome rest, I would have not agreed to a pause in journey.

Indeed, late that night, the run of freedom amid these unpermitted areas of the country met a hurdle. At a moment Linda and I were united in naked embrace, a knock came at the door of our hotel room.

I quickly clothed and opened the door, aiding the unwelcome entry of two females in uniform, either guards or police or soldiers. Linda gripped the bed covers, securing them under her chin. A prevailing arrogance possessed and protected me from any immediate concern, although it also inhibited any sign of respect on my part, despite the fact we were guests in the country. The officials demanded our passports and made it clear we were not allowed to be there. After delivering this clear message they turned and tramped out without closing the door.

In the morning a different set of uniformed officials arrived to ensure our compliance. They accompanied us to a bus that was to take us back in the direction from where we came. We obliged by taking a seat inside the vehicle. Though at the first sign of a stop to pick up further passengers, I told Linda I wanted to get out. She reluctantly agreed. Thus we stepped down, turned around and continued on our journey.

On the next night we had no alternative for accommodation as the bus we were on stopped at a single hotel beside the highway. This place housed far more rats than people. The massive rodents must have numbered in the 1 000s. It was a plague. The rodents were in the ceiling and in the room. The occasional individual somehow found its way on to our bed. The noise of scurrying feet did not abate throughout the night. There was little chance of sleep. Further, the bathrooms consisted of an outhouse where blood-covered newspaper lay strewn about and the toilets opened to a pigsty beneath where the huge animals awaited feeding. These experiences added further evidence in practical support of the government's regulation of foreign travellers' movements. This was becoming more than just uncomfortable.

What brought all of this activity to an end was a slow accumulation of a general fatigue. Further, I began to cough up a greasy substance that I guess was an accumulation of undigested low-quality cooking oil. An exit strategy was planned.

re-membering

We returned once again to Kunming, this time in order to arrange a more comfortable train trip up towards Chengdu in neighbouring Sichuan Province. From there we headed east and connected with the Yangtze River. At Chong Ching we bordered a boat and at Wuhan Linda departed to catch a flight back home. I continued down the river to Shanghai in the company of a European girl earning a living as an escort for moneyed Chinese businessman. From Shanghai to Hong Kong it was more boat transport, in fact, an ocean liner. After arrival there was no hesitation. I promptly made plans for onward travel.

∞

Ferdinand Marcos had been President of the Philippines since 1965. I was 2 years old at the time of his inauguration, and arrived in the country only days before he left, never to return, alive at least. Marcos reportedly profited billions from his country during his period in power, ordering much violence against those that appeared to stand in his way. Despite taking a keen interest in Asian affairs ever since the time I had hatched a plan to travel to this part of the world, I still had no idea of the gravity of the situation in the country at the time my feet touched the ground.

A revolution was underway. My curiosity inspired my first destination of interest, a trip to the Presidential Palace. It was intoxicating to be among the hordes of people gathered in protest. The entrance to the palace was blocked by razor wire, and behind it stood a line of armed soldiers interspersed with priests and nuns. The presence of the clergy, while quite a juxtaposition, was not totally surprising due to the country's overwhelming population of Catholics, and thus the authority these leaders of the church commanded. The atmosphere remained tense, however quite orderly despite the raucous crowd. Slogans were repeatedly chanted, obviously demanding the stepping down of the long-standing regime.

Suddenly, above the din, unmistakable sounds of rifle fire rung out and resonated. The crowd turned and quickly began to disperse. In the midst of the hysteria I too joined the stampede. In this situation I again felt no longer to be the individual I was brought up to believe I was. The notion of rights failed to have meaning. Within that dash there was no room for anything bar single-minded focus on survival. My legs kept pumping through the chaos.

The road ahead presented no less challenging than an obstacle course. The obstacles included humans running in multiple and changing directions, and more stationary objects such as poles, curbs, large drums, and, to my undoing, patches of low-lying razor wire. My legs got caught up and entangled in several strands and I fell to the ground. People propelling themselves directly behind me fell and trampled over me in their desperation to escape.

After the initial collisions, I had enough time and space to get back on my feet and untangle myself, although not before receiving several deep, long gashes to my shins. My new priority was to find some temporary shelter, a hiatus to rest and seek clarity within which I could weigh up my options. I noticed a number of people scurrying towards the entrance to a laneway on the other side of the road. I entered quickly, though slowed down after noting that it terminated as a dead end. A small crowd stood motionless at its extremity. I approached with caution, surveying the faces to try and gauge the mood. The reaction I received felt strangely dissonant. A number of the predominantly male congregation began to giggle. I faltered in my advance. I have no recollection of what happened next.

∞

I woke to, and perhaps as a result of, the feeling of a presence within my personal space. The presence felt warm, gentle, feminine. Upon slowly opening my eyelids, I beheld something of archetypal beauty. As my vision gained focus, it settled on the clean white and smooth brown contrast of a nurse leaning over my resting physique. Our eyes met, hers appeared as to scan for vital signs. I produced a small smile, which she returned. Appearing satisfied, she returned to an erect posture, exposing the presence of a second nurse at the foot of the bed.

The sound of occasional scattered rifle shots emanated from outside to my right. The shooting was close, but not so immediate to arouse concern. I felt relatively safe, reassured by the presence of the nurses, although resigned to any potential fate due to my relative physical incapacity and my ignorance regarding what was unfolding in the city surrounding me. I did not know if I was medicated, if so, it was not at a high dosage. The nurses left my side. I faded back into a deep sleep.

∞

With my leg wounds dressed and body rested, I was discharged the next day. There was wild celebration on the streets. I soon heard of the news that President Marcos had fled the capital by helicopter. I did not feel in the right frame of mind to join the jubilation. This had not been my battle. Further to my wounds, I self-diagnosed a mild trauma. I felt a stranger in a strange situation in a strange land. I returned to my guest house to rest in the hot and cramped dormitory I shared with one other guest and a number of mosquitoes.

Harel appeared to enjoy his own company, and this I mean quite literally. He embodied an enthusiasm with which he entertained, amused, and informed himself. He was very comfortable in his present incarnation, relaxed and joyful. His few possessions signalled not only a traveller of considerable experience, but also of clear mind.

We talked at great length as we reclined on our bunks. He, as I, approached this traveling adventure as an opportunity to advance personal experience and learning in so many ways. A book he availed for my perusal displayed evidence of the depths to his present investigations. Its opening pages described in simple terms the suffering inherent within a life ordinarily lived. It purported all suffering at its core to be symptomatic of seeking of some form. It went on to explain how life can be practised in a different way, recommending a radical non-seeking, regardless of the activity.

Soon after lending me this book for perusal, Harel's girlfriend turned up, reuniting the two after a long period of separation. The pair shared passionate embrace as they rolled around opposite me. It pleased me to view such playful intimacy. This was something I had not previously witnessed in the flesh.

In my formative years my impressions had been pre-dominantly forged through the viewing of my parent's dispassionate exchanges. Within my own experience, I had enjoyed sexual pleasure, although without so much mutual unconditional abandon, joy and childlike fascination as presently on display.

The degree of distracting activity this reunion caused resulted in the book loaned now inadvertently remaining in my keeping.

That evening I ventured out. I kept to the quieter thoroughfares, allowing space to relax and minimise undesirable interactions. Manila Bay provided untroubled ocean views to the west and a broad path upon which to walk along its shoreline. The path led on to Rizal Park, and to the monument of one of the country's heroes.

Reportedly a doctor of medicine, poet and artist, Dr. Rizal was executed on suspicion of inciting rebellion against the then Spanish colonising power. Whatever the actual circumstances, the execution exacerbated what became a revolution against the Spanish, only for the Americans to move in and take effective control for the next 50 years. The Philippines had not been a unified country before the Spanish arrived en route from Mexico. Consequently, the country was named after the ruling King of Spain of that time. The new country also embraced the Catholic religion of its colonisers, and remains significantly unified under this religious belief.

The park's extensive landscaped areas beckoned me deep within its interior. I eventually happened upon a café. The construction was of a square perimeter of counter that enclosed a preparation area. The outside of the counter was supplied with stools.

I sat on a corner stool several down from a man aged beyond his middle years. Though in contrast to his grey hair, the man's physique appeared strong, sinewy, his movements graceful in their efficiency. He exuded a sense of presence, of ambient awareness, as he poured over his English language newspaper.

With toothpick playing between his teeth, he glanced in my direction. His eyes smiled. He nodded an invitation to join him. I dismounted my stool and climbed on to the one opposite him.

Del had just returned from the airport where he had collected the most recent publications delivered through the agency of international arrivals. His interest was world affairs and how they relate to his country, his situation. Over the following few hours, he openly shared of his views on the present state of domestic matters, the corruption, the poverty, the environmental degradation at the hands of both the powerful and the poor.

I sat intently listening, as much absorbing his manner as attending to the details of his monologue. I had never before met such a person, someone of such worldly knowledge yet of a deeply relaxed disposition in spite of the troubling context such knowledge availed him, of grand vision though in acknowledgment of practical limitation, of passion though without expectation. He proceeded thoughtfully though without distraction, he articulated detail though remained cognisant of his audience, he remained inclusive though without solicitation, inviting though respectful. Del so ably embodied one version of how a personally meaningful life may appear.

We were soon joined by a group of local youths familiar to Del. They obviously respected his place within their lives, apparent from their system of verbal address and body language. These guys formed a collective that took care of each other. They shared their nights under the Manila sky among the palm trees within the park. The café owner provided safe storage of valuables for those that required it. This allowed for untroubled rest for whom the park had become a temporary home.

I was warmly invited to join them. On that day I declined, having already paid for accommodation in my hot and mosquito-friendly dormitory, though I related my delight to join them from the following day. This would also provide a leisurely amount of time to pack my possessions and prepare for the relocation.

∞

As a place to sleep, the park offered a level of comfort well beyond my prior expectation. It felt like as an oasis. The vast open space was consistently conditioned by a breeze blowing in from the bay. Fluttering coconut fronds dispersed the otherwise celestial panorama, forming an abiding shelter under which I bedded down. My numerous companions nurtured a confidence of security and peace of mind.

Since I was no longer paying for accommodation, I diverted my funds into subsidising daytime meals for the six or so guys with which I shared company. This turned out cheaper than the combined cost of previous accommodation and meals as a solo traveller.

Over the following weeks, Del and I continued our conversations while touring around the city. We visited both extremely rich and desperately poor areas. On a number of occasions Del mentioned an interest in providing developmental support to an island community off the coast of Subic Bay some 3 hours north of the capital. We made plans to visit the island so I could familiarise myself with the people and their situation.

In order to finance the trip, Del came up with a scheme through which I could sell my traveller's cheques on to an anonymous third party, claim them missing and thus receive a full refund. This resulted in the almost doubling of my finances, half of which I donated towards the funding of our venture. At the time this was not a concern for me as I harboured a perhaps not entirely justifiable disdain for big financial institutions with their focus on profiteering at any cost.

We were joined on the trip by another traveller, Jim, a young Canadian. He exhibited symptoms of an even more sheltered upbringing than my own through his self-consciously polite and conciliatory manner. The three of us set off by bus. Del suggested we make a stopover at the home of an American Evangelical Christian. The purpose of this visit wasn't clear to me, although Del was clearly on familiar terms with the guy.

Mike, a large framed, bellowing individual refrained from any specific reference to his beliefs until the following morning. At that time his powerful proselytising had a surprising impact on Jim, who fell to his knees and cried amid his parroting utterances of love for Jesus. Christianity nabbed another convert. One more willing to believe in what they didn't know, I thought. Prior to this Jim had appeared somewhat lost and vulnerable, though I was still surprised by his willingness to cede his authority so easily. The spectacle was admittedly unnerving. It was not that I was going to follow Jim's lead, but I may be pressured. It might become a confrontation. Ultimately it didn't come to that. When we moved forward in our journey however, it was without Jim.

Magalawa is a small island, no more than one kilometre at its widest stretch, and less than one kilometre from the mainland. The human population stood at about 200 at the time of our visit. I was told this number was mostly the product of nine families. The people were welcoming, though due to common language limitations, our interactions were limited to smiles and basic civilities.

Not long ago the island inhabitants were able to catch sufficient tuna to sustain themselves from the sea within close vicinity. A depletion of fish stocks led to expeditions further and further out in search of an adequate catch. These fleets of motorised outrigger canoes were now required to go beyond territorial waters and compete with the far superior technology of large Japanese fleets to gain a chance of bringing something home. The hunt for nutrition also led to the devastating introduction of dynamite to harvest what remained of fish around the island. Not only was the use of dynamite evidenced in the piles of shattered coral that washed up on the island's shoreline, but I also personally caught a blast at a moment my head was submerged during a swim, leaving my ears ringing for some hours. As combined catches diminished, malnutrition increased, especially among the very young, some of which had developed distended bellies.

Over time I settled in comfortably. The man with who Del did most of his communicating soon constructed a simple bamboo bed complete with mosquito net under his house for my use. While Del came and went while I remained. I preferred island life to the noisy and polluted Manila.

Negotiations continued during the times Del was around, the outcomes openly shared. We implemented Del's idea regarding snail culture, constructing a concrete enclosure for them. We also started to prepare an area for extended gardens along with a number of the island's female inhabitants.

During my frequent wanderings I developed a cut on the top of my long toe to which I initially paid little attention. However over time it demanded greater notice due to its enlargement. I thought the surrounding sea's saltwater may help with recovery but the wound continued to open. I tried various medicinal applications without positive results. By this time, it appeared that my bone may soon become exposed as the surrounding tissue continued to be eaten away. This called for more drastic measures. I sourced a military-grade application that came in a crystalline form and proceeded to fill the hole. Finally, a thin film of skin did grow over the wound and this began the long process of healing.

During the long periods of time I spent alone, I began to reflect upon my situation. I obviously had very little in common with the island's inhabitants, and had no answers to how I might spend my time more effectively. On occasion I took a canoe trip back to the mainland for novelty.

On one of these trips, after taking a bit of a hike around the coastal village port, I sat under a tree and waited for transport back to the island. There was a girl of around 20 years hanging around. We started up a conversation, which gravitated to the topic of ganja. She said she could supply me with some. After a brief hesitation, I agreed to a price to which she disappeared only to soon return with an ounce bag which I quickly concealed in my sack. Upon handing it over she warned I should be very careful. The tone of her voice was foreboding, rousing my suspicion.

Almost immediately following her words, two men in military uniform appeared from the other side of some shrubs, approached and aggressively inquired about the contents of my sack. One of the guys was armed with a rifle which he had pointed casually in the direction of my chest. By this time the girl had disappeared. One of the guys grabbed my sack, ripping the fabric and removing the bag of ganja. The situation enraged me. My anger exceeded any fear for the consequences. I demanded the armed man show some ID to prove his authority. I was surprisingly vindicated in my request when the guy produced a card with a stamp revealing his recent decommissioning as a soldier. I continued in my protests, they continued with nervous aggressive intent. The two men took a hold of me, one on each arm, and led me down the road. A crowd began to gather and follow.

re-membering

We arrived at a large building that looked like the offices of a civilian authority. Within a room on the ground floor I was sat down, my sack was confiscated and long conversations ensued between a man seated at a desk and the men in military uniform. After much discussion, a bag of marijuana was produced and I was asked if it was mine. The content of the bag was about half the amount I had received, and I told them so.

Over time people came and went, the crowd thinned, and then finally I was left alone with the man seated behind the desk. My sack was returned to me. I checked my wallet and found that it had been emptied of cash. I knew there was nothing I could do about the situation so I remained silent. I finally asked if I could leave to which the guy silently nodded.

The scale of complicity in what happened exceeded any ability I had to defend myself. What I hadn't fully considered was the relatively little value placed upon a life in this area of the world. In retrospect I concluded I had overrated my importance. My attitude surfaced as entitled behaviour. I feel now that preserving my life possibly meant little to nothing to those involved in the incident. There was perhaps not much reason why my life had been spared beyond a mere lack of utility in ending it. It was only a matter of a few weeks later when I heard rumour the mayor of that port settlement had been shot through the head.

By the time I was about half way back to the island, I noticed the presence of a large number of people on the beach. It looked like the entire community was waiting for me on the shore. News of the recent events had obviously preceded me. My concern shifted. It was no longer solely about the civilian and military authorities. I was now concerned more generally about who I was to these people. What started out as an experience in contribution to a cause of apparent value had now hoisted me onto centre stage. My life on the island was revealing itself to exist within the long shadows of not only institutionalised corruption, but also community expectations.

This level of combined pressure pushed hard against the front I had been previously presenting as of personal integrity. I became alarmingly aware of the pretences that had been guiding my actions. Now exposed, this facade could only crumble.

Behind this mask lay my ulterior motivations for being here. I clearly now saw I had been associating and identifying with this activity of broadly sanctioned virtue in order to display my life had meaning. I remember feeling chuffed as the story played out in my mind, how I was working for the betterment of the world. Now I saw I was primarily doing it for the purpose of constructing a positive self-image, not because I had a heart-felt desire to assist these people above all else. I had managed to fool myself, perhaps along with Del and the local community. This surrogate or fake identity had served to conceal the void that remained unfulfilled within me.

I had to get out of here. How was I going to extricate myself? It was the perfect nightmare. I was delivered under the guise of a supporting actor and now I was standing alone, front and centre, feeling naked and well out of my depth.

∞

Hong Kong was quickly becoming my crossroads. The days that followed my return held a mixture of great relief for my escape, confused feelings of guilt in relation to those I had left behind, and belatedly a returning sense of concern in terms of what to do now. The scenario that had unfolded in the Philippines, beyond its disillusionment, led on to much pondering regarding appropriate action given a perceived undesirable predicament. This was completely new territory. It was the first time I felt some responsibility in the lives of others. I had not thought it through. It unsettled preconceived notions of the very nature of what is good and bad, what is moral or ethical.

In the most general of terms, I could not clearly separate myself from the circumstances of the fishing community on the island of Magalawa. I too ate fish. I too formed a part of the overall pressure placed upon the planet's biological communities that supported the world's human population.

More specifically, remedying this most fundamental of concerns is obviously much bigger than an individual can attend. Further, the problem does not exist in isolation from the greater social politic. Corruption with its focus on personal gain was fundamental to the workings of day to day life as I'd experienced it. How is it possible for anyone to achieve anything of lasting value knowing who holds the power and the guns? It was a question felt best left unanswered at that stage. As yet I had no solution to offer the people I had walked away from.

The most fundamental of concerns resonated with unprecedented intensity. Underlying my willingness to involve myself in the lives of others had been an undeniable desperation to fill a personal vacuum. It exposed an essential flaw in my motivation.

The issue here was not in the details. Even if I had been granted the answers to the circumstantial challenges, it had become clear without heartfelt inspiration I could not truly succeed in any endeavour. Further, in acting with disingenuous purpose there was the unavoidable potential of unleashing all manner of chaotic repercussions. It did not appear to matter whether the action was inspired consciously or unconsciously. This fundamental truth appeared straight forward. I could not accomplish anything of value driven by ulterior motivations. This implied the existence of a heart as the source of all meaningful action.

Above all, the experience led to a refocusing of my efforts. Now the stakes had risen and my path had narrowed. It felt much closer to a matter of life and death.

My travel adventures so far had certainly added to my experience, although resolved little in terms of personal direction. Prior to the Philippines, much of my activities amounted to the observation of how others spent their lives, regardless of the culture, and this had quickly become an empty pastime. I had only really observed lifestyles not of my desire.

Most lifestyles appeared to be comprised of daily toil, in and around family, living within the bounds of constant prescription, doing things because that's what was expected, not because of all things considered, but because that is the way things had always been done. Prevailing systems worked to perpetuate and expand communities through the compiling of material resources. The consequences are hard work, competition, conflict and environmental destruction.

Individuals were so much an inextricable part of the group, and the group, of greater society. There existed a lack of personal sovereignty, a lack of ownership of actions, and thus a lack of responsibility. Co-operating in such social systems appeared to be a recipe for ignorance, resentment and unhappiness. Of course this kind of a life came with its excuses, its tolerances, but how does this corruption make up for the freedom that is lost, the freedom with which individuals maintain the ability to make personal choices and thus, most importantly, learn from the consequences of their actions? This inherited ground for choice-making is based upon questionable assumptions, that elders know better, that somehow we are all so identical in our vacuity that we should simply follow, and that this is a fulfilling lifestyle choice.

Here, the individual is not deemed sacred, not ultimately answerable only to themself. It may not even be assumed such individuals know of dreams, let alone how to go about their fulfilment. Humans are too busy satisfying the insatiable demands of their parents, partners and offspring. They are unlikely to learn of their contribution to this perpetuated folly as they lack the freedom and education and time to arrive at this conclusion. For those who stumble upon momentary insight, perhaps it is concluded as unacceptable to risk all by eschewing society's obligations. Is this a good enough reason to avoid an accurate contextual informing of the most important choices?

I desired more than what was on offer within these societies on display. I wanted a lifestyle that offered more than simply work in exchange for monetary compensation. Nothing I could buy would truly satisfy. Accepting the requirement to provide for material necessities, I yearned for a community that supported each other with love and sincerity as the priority modality, one that honoured the heart within all members. As yet I had not found an example of this. Why did such a place not exist? Surely I was not the only one for who this was desirable. Was I missing something?

∞

All the while my funds were dwindling. My thoughts began to turn to the possible necessity of returning to the country of my birth. The idea filled me with dread. It meant returning to the environment that I had fled.

The days that followed were passed alone. Daylight was spent close to nature from the seashores to the mountains. Here I could be alone with my thoughts. By night, I remained closer to my lodgings, visiting bookstores, researching all that may provide a lead.

I had been staying in a hostel since my return. Travelers came and went frequently. I was at times envious of their lack of a care beyond their next destination and who they may meet along the way. Though I knew this lifestyle could not satisfy me any longer.

I steered clear of these circles, and if at all, was more attracted to and mixed with the smaller group of individuals that remained for longer periods. It gradually emerged most of this smaller group were engaged in the export and import of a diversity of goods in and out of the territory, both legal and illegal. This was their means of support, but also their means of stagnation. My own lack of direction, increasing loneliness, and ultimately desperation, led to contemplating the option of getting involved in these activities. The idea of doing such a thing made me nervous, and my impressions of the various individuals who had previous experience did not alleviate my concerns. These guys seemed to be as directionless as I felt.

One evening while perusing inside a bookstore, I came across a work of interest. It presented detailed descriptive examples of the psychology of a normal life as a means of postulating the self-inflicted nature of its adversity. The content dovetailed with the literature I had been passed by Harel during our brief time together in Manila, though this contemporary work was more convincing in its direct relevance. The author was obviously a Westerner, as what he described resonated intimately with my own past.

After scanning the first twenty pages it became clear if I was to benefit from this information it was not going to be due to further reading. It had to be due to a radical shift in the very way I approached my moment to moment existence. Perhaps I was the source of my problems. I replaced the book on the shelf and left the store with resignation.

I continued in my solo wandering. I began to observe myself in the way recommended and understood from the literature. This practice of awareness became my priority and resulted in greater amounts of time spent simply sitting in the outdoors. I considered there was no benefit in seeking the company of others, but at the same time I yearned for it. I considered seeking the support of the Buddhist community, yet I had an aversion to what at that time I considered to be organised religion. I didn't want to be a monk. Surely there is nothing that necessarily changes simply because of an ordination, a head shaving and a change of clothes.

My daytime excursions had begun to take me further afield. Hong Kong's outer islands were now planned as destinations. The territory's impressively reliable public transport system made it convenient to get around. After arrival to the shore of the largest of these islands, I walked off the ferry and immediately began to climb the road that rose steeply from the shoreline. As in most locations, mountain roads are almost always of a series of serpentine curves, often with bridges crossing small streams that release water down the more shaded valley sections. This provides for pleasant trekking, albeit in ascent.

As I passed over one bridge I happened across a bearded Englishman. He did not appear to be on his way anywhere. He was also strangely without possessions, although this strangeness did not apply further to his character. Edward came across as quite the gentle man. His presentation and conversation suggested education and experience. To my surprise he explained this was his temporary residence, he sheltered and slept through the nights under this bridge. He too had walked away from an unsatisfactory life.

I informed him of my new found desire to find a contact within the Buddhist tradition in order to inquire about meditation. I was unsure of how to actually frame an explanation. I knew I yearned for understanding, and that my only leads were a couple of books. I wanted to proceed in a community of equally motivated individuals, and preferably in the presence of a mentor. He told me of a fellow countryman who was presently resident at Po Lam temple on the other side of the mountain. I sincerely thanked him and continued upon my winding walk up the mountainside.

It wasn't long before a small bus came into view during its slow ascent. I flagged the bus down. For the first time in a while I had a place to go, something to accomplish. The bus carried me along the at times very narrow road to Po Lin temple at the top of the mountain. To get to Po Lam I would need to continue down the other side of the peak.

Upon alighting at the final stop, I looked up and felt glad that Po Lin was not my destination. This temple was a popular tourist spot and clearly well financed. This was easily seen in its adornments, their lavishness, the shininess of the gold and silver. The monks here formed a part of the attraction, and this bothered me. I was approaching this institution from a past rejecting the accumulation of material possessions as something ultimately devoid of joy, seeing temples as a place where the true value of a life may be nurtured. This temple did not escape the veneration of the material, on the contrary it appeared to attract it.

From the bus stop the onward journey was by pedestrian path. The path wound down on its way to a small fishing village. This environment encouraged positive feelings about my destination. The path quickly left the noisy worshipping atmosphere and ushered me back into the relative quiet of natural surrounds. The way was flanked by long grass, in contrast to the tall forests on the side of the island I had ascended. This was clearly the drier side. The view was idyllic, uninterrupted, consisting of the grey-green of the mountainside sloping gently towards the glistening deep blue of the ocean that separated the island from the Chinese mainland. As I walked, my mood continued to improve. The gentle slope made for an ease of walking. Wisps of breeze occasionally caressed my face and caused the seeding grasses to sway as one.

Po Lam temple was situated about half way down. It presented a different setting to the temple at the top of the mountain. It was located at a sufficiently inconvenient distance to deter tourists and their habituated lives of comfort. The place was actually a nunnery. The nuns were gardeners. The area developed for the production of food was sizeable, and well-tended.

The sound of chattering female voices was my first sign of human presence and it was this to which I was attracted in order to seek information. There was an absence of English speakers among the few nuns in the garden, although they understood when I mentioned the name Alec. They repeated the name with approval and urged me to the building that stood opposite the main temple.

I walked up to the entrance nearest and called out for Alec. 'Yeah?' came the immediate rising tone of the welcome. The voice came from inside a cubicle-like room at the corner of the larger space at the entrance to which I stood. Without any pause Alec threw the interior door open and approached, inviting me inside with a graceful hand gesture. He was dressed in informal grey clothing, as a practitioner of karate might wear. The jacket was closed by a thick sash of similar colour, though did not completely conceal a large tattoo on his chest. He was a short man, but of thick build. His head had been recently shaved in keeping with the tradition of a monk's life.

Alec arrived in Hong Kong a number of years previously after a period of dissatisfaction with his life in England. He admitted to having issues with anger that landed him in trouble at times, and he decided something needed to be done about it as a priority. Ultimately he determined the situation was important enough to warrant leaving his homeland and committing to a monk's life. He lived here most of the year, although travelled to Japan during the winter retreat season.

At the first opportunity I briefly recounted my search and experiences that had led me to a resignation and now the temple. After standing quietly through my reporting, Alec responded with an offer to arrange an introduction to the abbot. He managed this without delay, and through his capable Cantonese translation I heard the granting of permission to join the community at Po Lam. This result was however provisional upon permission of, and therefore a visit to, Hong Kong immigration.

∞

Perhaps due to the unusual nature of my request, the immigration officials appeared doubtful of the authenticity of my stated purpose. The facial expressions and physical gestures that accompanied their considerable deliberations led to this clear impression. It dawned on me that, amid the black market-rampant, business-centric atmosphere of this territory, my type of appeal may prompt suspicion, casting me as a possible fugitive, a criminal seeking a place to hide perhaps.

The sole female informed me of their need to contact the temple. She ultimately was able to converse with the abbot who, she explained with a grin, had confirmed my story and his permission. I was allowed back but there remained an issue as Hong Kong did not normally allow for foreign layman to be resident in Buddhist temples indefinitely.

The situation was not ideal. Alec, being a monk ordained in the local order, did not share my problem. He suggested I inquire at a temple in Japan where he had regularly stayed as a base between periods of formal retreat. I immediately sat down and wrote a letter. Without further delay I ascended the path to Po Lin temple and the public post box on the side of the road.

$$\infty$$

Meanwhile Po Lam's annual 3-month period of winter retreat was drawing to a close. During sitting sessions, the entire temple community shared a bench that ran almost the entire interior wall of the main temple building, only interrupted to allow space for the main entrance doors that stood in the middle of opposing walls.

The males sat together. I was situated next to Alec, and he in turn next to the abbot. To my left sat a young Hong Kong Chinese guy. The gathering otherwise was made up entirely of nuns, over twenty of them. We all sat in silence, facing towards the large golden Buddha statue in the centre of the room.

There were breaks between sessions for vegetarian meals. The nuns responsible for food preparation were competent chefs. Beyond the meals, certain nuns also busied themselves with the making of tofu from soya beans supplied to the temple in large sacks. There was a large variety of products prepared from the liquid derived through the crushing of the rinsed beans between a pair of large stones that formed a manual press.

I contributed to the day to day life of the temple by cutting the long dry grass growing at the edge of the mountain path. This maintained the verges in a tidy condition and also provided fuel for the kitchen stoves. I learnt from some of the nuns of how to use a sickle, bundle and tie the grass with a few of the cut strands, skewer the bundles on to each end of a bamboo pole, and to finally carry them down the hill on foot.

How long had humans toiled in this manner with these tools? For someone who was dedicating themselves to a meditative lifestyle, the work was ideal.

∞

I soon received a response from Japan. I was welcome to go and practice as a layman. I organised a one-way plane ticket. This purchase left me with just enough funds to cover my transport to the airport and the onwards train fare beyond touching down in Japan.

seclusion's revelations

I was educated to believe my country was up with the front runners in human technological development. Even before walking out of Tokyo's international airport, indications were Japan was more advanced.

I had never before beheld so much automation, from machines supplying a bewildering variety of products to communication devices exhibiting innovation of previously unheard-of convenience. After exiting the terminal, I boarded a train that quickly accelerated to a speed more rapid than I had previously experienced from this form of transport. I had heard about the country's bullet train, but this was not it, this was merely a suburban connection. On the final leg of my journey, from the station to the temple on foot, I passed more machines, some supplying alcohol, mainly beer, but also sake and other stronger liquors. These installations displayed Japan as not only more technologically advanced, but also more socially sophisticated. In Australia such dispensers would be surely regularly smashed and plundered, and thus not be a viable option.

It was after dark by the time I arrived at Hakuhoji (白峯寺 - white peak temple). The entrance drive was unlit. I as much felt my way along with the help of the moonlight reflecting off the white and grey gravel. Large panes of glass constituting the side of a large building ran parallel and to my right. Before long, this building recessed into a courtyard, one side of which housed a set of generous sliding doors, left wide open. This entrance was also shrouded in darkness. Further, there was no sound. The silence contrasted the baseline ringing within my ears.

I felt I had reached the right place. My surroundings indicated this to be the central thoroughfare. I stood reluctant to call out, lest I disturb some ongoing meditative activity. As peaceful as the atmosphere was, I remained focused on the task at hand, to secure at least some shelter on this chilly evening. I decided it was enough to stay in this general vicinity and wait for the time being. At times I meandered off to reassure myself of my choice of location, though I limited these forays to a distance within which I could still stay in touch with any signs of movement in and around the previously discovered doorway.

Finally and suddenly, interior to the main doors, one side of yet another pair of sliding doors was flung open in one sharp motion. Interrupting the soft light that had escaped this opening, a bald man in a black robe and brown sash emerged and made his way intently to a single wooden stair, slipped into slippers, and moved out. He passed by with head down and without acknowledgement, turning and making his way down the gravel drive away from the direction I had originally entered. At the far end of the drive, he slid open a door to a building on the opposite side and disappeared within.

More monks filed out through the sliding doors the first individual had left open. One of them approached with a grin providing me the opportunity to explain my presence. He nodded his head as I quietly talked, providing some indication he had been informed of my impending arrival. His introduction as Shoko San reminded me of the name that had signed off on the reply to my original correspondence.

An elderly man soon approached on the request of Shoko San. He was introduced as Hojo San, the abbot of the temple. He welcomed me jovially, his simple English punctuated with effortless laughter, the expression of which required little more breath than for his calm vocalisations.

Shoko San invited me to supper. After downing my pack in the foyer, I followed around the back of an ascending wooden staircase, through more sliding doors, and into the bright lights of a kitchen, the first room not of traditional design. The long central stainless bench spoke of utility beyond tradition, utility with quantity in mind. At this bench I was invited to sit.

Monks and laymen arrived, dropped onto stools beside and across from where I sat, in front of wherever a large bowl of steaming noodles had been placed. Alongside each bowl of noodles were further smaller bowls, one of soup broth, one of slivered leeks.

I followed the lead of my new community members. After combining the simple ingredients, alternatively using chopsticks to lift strands of the thick white noodles to my mouth and raising the bowl to drink of its liquid, eating was accomplished. The local monks appeared to vacuum each helping of long noodle strands into their mouths and slurp from the broth in a single combination of movements. I did not mirror them. I did not know how. The vacuuming technique seemed to be driven by the diaphragm. It was accompanied by an unrestrained siphoning sound as the noodle strands quickly vanished between lips. In this way supper proceeded unceremoniously. Bowls were emptied of their contents in minutes, then carried to a deep sink where they were given a quick rinse before being left upturned to drain on the bench opposite. All departed in the way they had arrived and ate, noisily and without a word.

After supper, Shoko San showed me upstairs and hence back into the realm of traditional form. We passed through a smoothly sliding light wood-framed door, one of a set that together constituted the entire width of dividing space between interior rooms. We walked upon tatami rice straw matting that provided a gentle spring to each step. Wooden-framed shoji-papered sliding panels concealed outer windows and filled the middle wall space. A mattress roll was extracted from a set of floor level cupboards that ran the length of the room. The mattress, co-operatively unfurled, revealed bed covers appropriate to the cold weather.

Shoko San disappeared, soon to return holding a type-written schedule of the temple's daily activities:

Daily timetable			
4.00 – 6.00	zazen	(座禅)	sitting zen
6.00 – 6.40	chanting	(お経)	
7.00 – 7.30	cleaning		
7.30	breakfast		
9.00 – 11.00	samu	(作務)	productive service
12.00	lunch		
2.00 - 4.00	samu		
4.00	bathing		
6.00 – 8.00	zazen		
8.00	supper		

re-membering

Zen activities and the terms that refer to them share a local history that stretches back over half a millennium. The spirit of these practices reverberates and maintains a broad, long-standing influence throughout the culture. Well known examples of Zen-inspired arts include the tea ceremony (茶道) and calligraphy (書道), and the martial arts including judo (柔道) and swordsmanship (武士道). All of these disciplines are identified with the same final written character, its literal translation denotes a way or path. This not only points to all such disciplines as means to a specific mastery, it suggests many ways to a more essential universal realisation. Practically speaking, all these activities provide the ground for understanding the nature of the self through exhaustively engaging within the given activity.

In this way, Zen has inspired and nurtured the development of some of the most unique of cultural characteristics, constituting a fundamental contrast between East and West. This makes translation between the languages on such matters difficult to impossible, providing the potential of misunderstandings among Western practitioners of Japanese fine and martial arts.

Translated into English, the term 'Zen' is unavoidably subject to the limiting ideas within the history of English language culture. Emanating from its strongest influences of Christianity and reductionist science, the culture of the West is structurally dichotomous in its outlook. It is founded on unquestioned separation between subject and object, self and other, us and them, organism and environment, god and humanity. It creates for itself a world of opposing conditions and spurious connection, success and failure, winning and losing, presence and absence, cause and effect, good and bad.

This renders the culture an essential tension, and leaves it silent in its ability to define the nature of Zen. By way of example, Zazen or sitting Zen, perhaps finds its most popular translation in the word 'meditation,' though meditation suggests an activity undertaken by someone with some aim or purpose. Zazen, on the other hand, elucidated through its parent term 'shikantaza' (只管打坐), literally means 'nothing but sitting.' It is objectless in space and intention.

Perhaps greater ease of comprehension may be found by examining stories that emerged from the Zen lineage. It is well known that Buddhism arose and spread out of Northern India, emanating through the life and teachings of Gautama. What is lesser known is that the essence of the teaching reached China through the transmission of patriarchs by the end of the 6th century, and further, became known to Huineng, the 6th Chinese patriarch around the end of the 7th century. It is Huineng that is often credited with the origin of Chan (Zen).

The story of Huineng is one of a poor wood seller, an uneducated layman, who, upon hearing a recitation of the Diamond Sutra, a now well-known Buddhist text, immediately realised his own essential nature. This began the school of instant enlightenment. Previous to this there had been a practice, a method, a process over time followed in order to lead to this realisation. Now Zen was presenting all as already enlightened, just ignorant of it.

The tale of Huineng is a powerful reminder of untapped and boundless potential present within the individual. There may be many numbers of schools with many numbers of teachers, and yet it only takes one being to embody another more direct way to displace all of tradition. Instant enlightenment meant that through the Zen tradition, Buddhism had evolved a school of no teaching, no path, a methodless method. It became better known as a tradition of direct transmission, person to person. Dogen brought this understanding and practice back to Japan during the 13th century and continued its conveyance.

re-membering

∞

I woke up as arranged, through the rousing of a fellow layman. At just before 4 am it was still dark, and cold. I put on the thin comfortable clothing I had sewn together during my time in Hong Kong and made my way downstairs. I trailed my fellow layman into the Zen Hall. Beyond the characteristic tatami matting and shoji rice paper screens, the singular addition of a calligraphy-inscribed painting hung in a small alcove at the far end of this otherwise spartan enclosure. Emptiness abounded.

Bowing upon entry. Walking to the rear of one of many large cushions. Bowing once more. Sitting on the cushion facing the wall. Positioning a further small round cushion under the buttocks to raise the torso. Folding the legs, each foot above each opposite thigh. Straightening the upper body. Uniting left and right hand, finger tips touching corresponding finger tips. Sitting in stillness. The sound of a resonating bell, time's only reference. Rising to slow intent steps around the exterior of the room. Further sitting. The resonating bell.

Zazen's sitting posture is referred to as the full lotus position. This is not a posture that everyone can easily achieve, although when managed provides a tripod-like strength conducive to long periods of sitting. This position is something I had performed as a child, in preparation for a playful stunt of walking across a carpeted floor on my knees.

From the outset of my formal practice at the temple, I informed my mindfulness through the central premise of the literature sourced through my travels, being that personal activity of all types tends commonly to seek an outcome of some sort, and all such seeking results in suffering of some sort, so do not seek. The suggested practice is to witness the constant seeking that goes on in the mind, and therefore understand how suffering is self-made.

I got the idea, past experience aligned with the message. Seeking can indeed produce a sense of lack. What I didn't understand is the extent to which all phenomena, everything that arises, tended to be associated with seeking. The hearing sense sought beauty in the call of a bird, the sense of touch sought remediation in its scanning for any clue of discomfort, the nose sought for signs of lunch readiness. Upon recognising these tendencies, seeking within the mind is claimed to cease, revealing within this space original unconditional mind. I continued my observations with increased vindication and zeal.

Chanting followed morning Zazen in the Hondo (the main hall). Chanting, nothing but chanting, pure and simple. This is a boisterous session of deep guttural sound powered by the diaphragm, set to the rhythmic thud of a wooden gong. It is a grand celebration, expressing the wisdom of, and deep gratitude for, past patriarchs, those that kept alive and transmitted this esoteric teaching throughout the ages. Cleaning followed chanting, breakfast followed cleaning, and then a rest before samu, beginning with the maintenance of the temple's gardens.

Zen temple gardens are world famous for good reason. They represent a unique and significant cultural inheritance from the Orient's ancient past. Their history can be traced as far back as the Chinese Daoist immortals said to have lived in perfect harmony with nature, onwards through the national religion of Shinto and its reverence for the great dignitaries of the nature spirits, present within the rocks, the trees, the rivers, within all things, and on to Buddhism with its focus within garden composition and arrangement on the incitement of original mind within the viewer.

These various though inseparable influences manifest themselves through miniaturised interpretations of nature, their well-known large rock installations and river-like gravel swirls, and sculpted trees featured to represent natural forces at play, the impact of the elements, and the ageing influence of time. Landscapes borrow from the natural surrounds, suggestive of a seamless continuum between the wild and the designed. Asymmetry contrasts horizontal and vertical elements, water and bamboo, buildings and boulders, further highlighting the nature of and within.

These gardens triggered the consciousness cannabis had briefly previewed within me. Resonating the strongest was the direct experience of a world alive and intelligent, known to itself throughout its respective parts and its numinous whole. There is something unifying within the mix, some force that ran through everything.

This seminal experience was all I had to proceed with for so long. It was the only suggestion of meaning that I had found of sufficient integrity. Thus I had nurtured it as a priority, as dull and distracted as I sometimes became. This I had carried through my more than one year of travel. Now standing with tools in hand, excitement peaked at the opportunity to contribute to the maintenance of this inspirationally indicative quasi-artifact.

Around the temple's main buildings traditional gardens were well established. A pond of brightly coloured carp stood as a central feature, refreshed by recycled water entering after winding its way through a pure stand of thick, well-spaced bamboo. Cloud trees abounded, pruned and shaped, hydrangeas huddled within the understory, and sakura trees lined the main entrance way. A collection of zoned cemeteries spread out beyond the temple's built environment, expanding in response to society's incessant need for space to house the ashes of its ancestors. In Japan all deceased relatives are cremated by law with the exception of the emperor. For most, temples are the place where the body is burnt and its ashes stored. At Hakuhoji, individual family sites were commonly constructed of fine imported marble, and decorated through the addition of a pair of dwarfed coniferous trees.

Samu was a joyful activity. No one told me what to do, in stark contrast to my childhood. Beyond the morning rush for bamboo brooms to sweep the main driveway, no one else significantly involved themselves in the temple's upkeep. I was delighted to move around and discover whatever appeared as in most need of attention.

A seasonal cycle emerged. In summer weeding and grass-cutting remained a full-time activity. Autumn presented an opportunity for pruning trees, shrubs and hedges. Large trees occasionally required the lopping of branches to prevent overcrowding and to maintain clear passage ways. Smaller trees required shaping to maintain their original intended form. Winter often brought snow and thus became a time for extensive cleaning of the building interiors, rooms dusted from top to bottom and shoji paper replaced. Spring presented an opportunity for maintenance, preparing for the growing season, a time aptly beautified through the blooming of the cherry trees. Year round, windows required cleaning. At times the abbot entertained guests, often businessmen, to whom green tea was served.

Bowing. Walking to the cushion. Bowing. Sitting on the cushion. Positioning the further round cushion to raise the torso. Folding the legs. Straightening the upper body. Uniting left and right hand. Stillness…………………………The sound of a resonating bell. Rising to slow intent steps. Sitting……………………….The resonating bell.

It was several days in to my residency when the fundamental realisation made itself known. The experience was subtle, but unmistakable, subtle yet crystal clear, subtle yet utterly relieving, subtle and blissful. There it was between the arising of discrete forms. In the absence of anything identifiably personal, there was no identifiable person. There is no separate me. Still I am, within the presence, though presence in the absence of separateness, presence that is consciousness, as of all things. This presence has no inside or outside.

This had not only been personally previously overlooked or forgotten, within my native culture there also existed practically no reference or indication of this most essential knowing. There was an almost total absence of language to describe it. I had never known the word 'self' to include all. Within the English language, the self is only ever referred to as something that is separate, and thus distinguishable from its environment.

It was not accurate to refer to what was happening as an experience either, as generally an experience is a phenomenon attributed to an individual within relative circumstances. There was no separate individual nor external environment. My native culture was founded upon an illusionary separation, and thus indeed, its tongue is forked. This refound, recast, recontextualised everything, not just the nature of self and experience. This dissolving resolved everything.

re-membering

In attempting to make something of it, to maintain this as an experience, to keep it going, the insight disappeared. I soon realised I was seeking again, and suffering through a sense of lack, again. I proceeded to sit with renewed abandon, without trying to achieve any outcome, within unconditional relationship. I continued in vigilance, inquiring of any avoiding behaviour that arose. I maintained this practice at all times, while sitting and while not sitting.

Bowing. Walking to the cushion. Bowing. Sitting on the cushion. Positioning the further round cushion to raise the torso. Folding the legs. Straightening the upper body. Uniting left and right hand. Stillness. The sound of a resonating bell. Rising to slow intent steps. Sitting. The resonating bell.

Hakuhoji is a temple with a history of over 400 years. The large Gingko trees situated at the front of the main hall at an average girth of some 4 metres stand in testimony to this considerable longevity. The patriarch's graveyard accommodates around 20 headstones, testimony to the lineage of men who had been in residence in that capacity since the beginning.

Being of its age, the temple would have had its origins at the beginning of the Edo period. During this era the capital began its shift from Kyoto to the location of present-day Tokyo, within the region of which Hakuhoji was built. By that time there had been little Western cultural influence in the country, with the exception of the zealous evangelism of a small number of mainly Portuguese Christian missionaries prior to its eventual bloody outlawing. My own country had as yet not seen white settlement.

At the time of its inception, the outlook from the temple's hilltop location would have primarily been one of rice paddies. The view through my eyes was one of a recently established sub-urban community. The vista of homogeneous modern abodes formed part of an outward growth of accommodation and commercial enterprise that had sub-sumed the port city of Yokohama on its way from the capital 40 kilometres away.

A temple increasingly surrounded with local community is a temple increasingly called upon to serve its community function. This distinguishes village temples from mountain temples; the latter tend to dedicate more of their time to formal Zen practice.

Hojo San let me know early his was a village temple, and he is a businessman. It was explained to me he had previously run a jewellery retail in Ginza, the area of Tokyo commanding some of the highest land values not only in the capital, but the entire world. An illness that resulted in the regurgitation of blood kept him sitting upright at night and eventually led him to temple life.

He managed the temple as no less a business. An office within the grounds took care of the purchase of gravesites; negotiated the design of graves within which the ashes of family members were placed in individual urns; and offered a selection of fine imported marble as construction materials. A pet cemetery was added and became very popular during the duration of my stay. There were chanting services provided on request, especially on days of importance within the Buddhist calendar.

I was told it takes a year's average wage to pay for a family site at a temple. The combined profitability of temples throughout the country reportedly rivalled the country's top 10 industries of that period. All the while Buddhist temples enjoyed tax-free status as do many of the world's religious institutions.

Of course, where there is money there are those attracted to it, intent on gaining a share of the spoils. At Hakuhoji it was no secret that a number of monks were in expectation of the gifting of a temple to call their own through Hojo San's agency. Tokugen San, the senior monk, was already in line to take over at Hakuhoji once Hojo San had passed. This meant if the other monks wanted to have a temple of their own, they would need to rely on the boss's generosity. During the duration of my stay this issue arose and fell seemingly cyclically, though no one appeared to move any closer to that inheritance.

After a while I too began to benefit from the temple's considerable wealth generation. Hojo San began to provide an allowance in the form of cash sealed in a brown envelope and delivered within the generosity of his gown's draping sleeves. I felt greatly appreciative. It allowed for a replenishment of my depleted funds.

Bowing. Walking to the cushion. Bowing. Sitting. Positioning the further cushion. Folding the legs. Straightening the upper body. Uniting left and right hand. Stillness.   The sound of the bell.   Rising. Slow   intent   steps.   Sitting. The resonating bell.

To my minimal understanding, a culture can emerge, survive and thrive through a number of uniquely evolved configurations of attributes, as long as these combine successfully over sufficiently long periods of time. At least, a culture needs to provide itself the necessary resources to nourish it, protect against environmental extremes, defend against intrusion, and maintain internal and thus social cohesion. Within the limits of necessary co-operation, the citizenry within any given human culture may perceive itself in relation to other in ways that vary significantly.

From a Western perspective, Japanese society displays stark contrast. As my stay expanded, it was with less certainty that I viewed the citizens as individuals, as opposed to as part of a greater harmonised collective functioning as one, as an individual. My increasing experiences with the local population revealed them as of such a primarily national identification. Most Japanese are guided through life beginning with a Shinto ceremony a month after birth, passing through marriage in a Christian Church, and finally cremation in a Buddhist temple. This mixture of traditions reflects a society unbeholden to one exclusive religious institution.

I was most commonly and earnestly asked of my impressions of the country. It always felt that a negative response would be received as a personal criticism. On the rare occasions I talked with individual monks, there was often obvious pride on display regarding all things Japanese. Stories became fairly imaginative at times, including the insistence that Jesus had visited Japan during his lifetime, and that foreigners are incapable of achieving enlightenment. Though nobody uttered a personal boast, nor fished for personal compliments. An identification first and foremost as Japanese appeared to free the locals into an unabashed elicitation of praise for the country as an indirect means of feeling personal adulation. Perhaps this avoids the risk of the accusation of personal boasting.

The temple community, like communities in general, ebbed and flowed through periods of calm and colourful drama among and within its factions. Beyond the occasional traditional ceremony, the majority monks passed significant amounts of time free, a fraction of them within a carpeted television room of sofas and stale cigarette smoke. Occasional drunken bouts spilled into the local neighbourhood courtesy of the more youthful, both ordained and not as yet, once resulting in some vehicle damage, more regularly furthering irredeemable notoriety towards the temple community. Differences sometimes led to tensions and the surfacing of harboured prejudices that further infected the social chemistry.

George, a hard-working Irish layman of some 40 years, often angered as he talked of the laziness of which he accused the monks. There was even the occasional flare up between a Westerner and one of the Japanese laymen. Once it came to the smashing of glass, although nothing major became of this nor of other incidents of similar magnitude. No-one was evicted and tensions quickly simmered down.

Involvement in such extraneous interactions were always optional. Within the tradition it is appropriately acceptable to spend days in silence and transport to and fro with head down, sharing little conversation, let alone disagreement.

Bowing. Walking. Bowing. Sitting with upright posture. Uniting hands. Stillness. The sound of the bell. Rising. Slow intent steps. Sitting. The resonating bell.

Love is one of those words that has been abused increasingly in this era of commodification. The word remains a powerful incantation, and one easily exploited commercially. I don't comfortably promote usage of the word in any context short of the unconditional. The notion of one loving another is fraught with confusion due to its relative impossibility, and thus the utterance of the term remains of questionable motivation.

Its sentimental reference implies emotional investment in a personal romantic vision featuring a caricature of an other and mistaken as this other. Fundamental problems arise from this situation as the other will inevitably not remain equal to that vision and thus is destined to act in ways that lead to the triggering of self-inflicted disappointment within the vision-holder. This drama and its consequence is so common it is arguably the norm. Mostly it is simply a matter of degree. Repercussions may be lifelong. Regardless, many are repeatedly attracted to this definition and expression.

It is clear the only love there can be is that which resides within, as and of itself, love that is unlimited in time and space. It does not change and does not relate to any specific individual. This love is rather a way of being, a source from and through which to act. It can be realised through a re-membered unity or non-duality. This love treats all as self. To understand its true nature is to cleanse relationship of significant misunderstandings, and thus to resolve a significant cause of otherwise unavoidable related suffering.

Thus, I couldn't say I loved the abbot of Hakuhoji temple. What I can say is within his vicinity, within his house, my awareness of love emerged. He presented as the first person of sufficient trust-worthiness for me to develop the confidence to utterly let go into the acceptance of all. In this way I re-opened the ground for love to be re-discovered. This opening birthed tears of joy, and facilitated an ongoing propensity. Once re-discovered, I was able to move within this boundlessness. In retrospect I understand there is perhaps no requirement for another to motivate such openness. This is simply how it happened for me.

Bowing. Walking. Bowing. Sitting. Uniting hands and, ...stillness. The sound of the bell. Rising. Slow intent steps. Sitting.   The resonating bell.

Winter was sesshin (接心) season, the period of the year when many of the monks went off to retreat at a mountain temple. Traditionally, monks sat for long hours in the winter due to it being convenient to stay indoors away from the snow and the cold. Without exception, the monks and laymen of Hakuhoji frequented a small temple in the vicinity of Kyoto, Hosshinji (発心寺 - temple of awakening). The temple was not the draw, the teacher was. As the story goes, this man was sitting within a jet fighter's cockpit ready for his kamikaze mission the very moment the emperor declared the surrender which brought an end to the second world war.

Sesshin ran with an intense sitting schedule, day and night. A monk charged with keeping all sufficiently sharp moved silently down the aisles between sitting cubicles armed with a long piece of planed timber. This tool was used to slap sitters across the shoulders if found slumping. Sitters could request a strike by bowing.

The teacher would visit the Zen Hall once a day to deliver a monologue, although these were never translated into English, and, at the time of visitation, my Japanese language skill was insufficient to facilitate sufficient understanding. Suffice to say it was clear from his tone that we should be urgent in our pursuit in this rare opportunity. Compulsory individual teacher interviews were also held daily, conducted with the same intensity.

This kind of format is so seductive to so many. We are brought up to believe we need to work hard on achievement. We are brought up to accept external authority without question to this end. We are brought up to accept externally imposed discipline to this end. All this is clearly on display at sesshin. Immersed in such culturally iconic activities, rituals and practices, it is seductive to believe something is being achieved, that there is personal development happening.

re-membering

This belief was evidenced in the air of arrogance that surrounded a number of the monks and layman on their return from session. This is the problem with externally-driven motivation and effort. Also, where there is external authority and imposed discipline there is its unavoidable periodic absence. Where there is effort there is also downtime. Yet from what is true there is no leave. And the truth remains equally accessible for those who prefer to relax, laugh and frolic.

Bowing.   Walking.   Bowing.   Sitting.   Stillness.
The sound of the bell.   Slow intent steps.   Sitting.
The resonating bell.

Over the months and several years, I spent longer and longer sitting within the vastness of my mind. This emptiness contains all things and knows no meaningful boundary, knows no time. Within the Zen Hall, sitting, the bell, an hour and 40 minutes passes within a single moment. It was with Hojo San that I often shared these prolonged sits, present within the bliss which is my, his, our essence.

Bowing. Walking. Bowing. Sitting. Stillness……

…..was it that the bottom fell out or the top blew off, or did the sides give way, or all, or none? Was it explosion or implosion, or both, or neither? It all happened so fast, lightning fast, beyond describe-ability, beyond comprehension, and then … this. I found myself as the presence within the room, simultaneous to being the presence outside it. I could hear all that was arising everywhere within consciousness, though I wasn't actually hearing it, I was it. The centre of all things was everywhere, and it was my centre. What formerly identified as self, the fickle thinker, now fragmented, minuscule, weak and desperate, willed the body to flight.

Flee to where? An idea desperately sought refuge. Where is Hojo San? In this moment he was absent from the Zen Hall. The mind's eye birthed an image of his form, laughing heartily in response to my pointless pleas.

I stood the body without the accustomed reverence, stumbled as if drunk, threw open the door, dropped beyond the step, fumbled with shoes, tottered onwards through the entrance, coming to rest on the drive. Inherent knowledge filled entire space, contextualising and overwhelming remnants of diehard suggestions of thought.

All fell silent. Within the infinite space existent as mind, transparent properties were now clearly discernible. I am all things and all things are love and loved. I am all things and all things are known, known to and as self. Tears flowed, self-worth unmistakably re-discovered and acknowledged, all steps to this point recognised as perfect, multiple emotions coalesced in their outflowing. Here, suffering is impossible, life and death an illusion. This could not die. It had never been born. There is possibly more than this, but nothing further necessary. No teacher required, no student to be. There was nowhere to go and nothing to do, and this only to be done. Of course, I remember this! I had been here before. In fact I had never left.

Will tentatively straightened the body into an upright posture. There was no need to move from one point within to another point within. I moved a couple of steps. What to do where there's nothing to do, where omission too is action? This was now the irrelevant question, if I ever felt the need to entertain one. Everything meant nothing and nothing meant everything.

Why meditate? Meditate on what?

re-membering

∞

I ceased my schedule. Hojo San moved to a house in the suburbs. I asked him without conviction, in the absence of anything else, about ordaining as a monk. He laughed. He suggested I establish a Zen Centre with him in Australia. What was there to teach? I packed my bag.

re-membering

re-membering

part 2

the vehicle

re-membering

re-membering

training may grant vehicular knowledge inside and out

tho' this does not comprehensively inform of driving,

with how much abandon and how much caution,

at what speed, in which gear, and at what stage to brake?

to which destination, and by which combination of roads?

on the contrary vehicular knowledge may distract from means and ways of destination arrival

it may lead to unguided trips to nowhere, circle work

re-membering

the bubble

My flight to Australia stopped over in Thailand. I planned to take advantage of this opportunity and spend some time on the islands after years in the temperate climate and semi-urban environment within which the temple was located. I took with me a determination to maintain a conscious awareness, a will to dwell as and within the freedom of presence. This would be assisted by a measured pace and a simplicity of movement.

In keeping with this strategy, I took temporary rest within the unique urban sprawl that is Bangkok. The accompanying inconvenience was not ideal, however in the absence of necessary arrangements to facilitate ongoing travel, it would do for a short time.

It only became clear after arrival back into the world of many choices that my years in a cloistered environment had relinquished some of my previous familiarity and preference for Western culture. I found myself searching for a surrogate for what I had most recently adopted as home. I gravitated towards China town.

My study of the Japanese written language had armed me with an understanding of many of the old pictorial representations that had originated in mainland China. Though the mainland Chinese were now using simplified characters, these innovations did not affect the populations of dispersed expatriate Chinese and their descendants who by now had been living outside their ancestral home for centuries.

For perhaps reasons similar to my own, the place I stayed attracted predominantly Japanese guests, both old and young, the older all male, the younger a mix of genders, although still mostly male. The older men tended to a solitary existence. More than one admitted they would not endure a return to their country of birth. In the culture within which all is arranged through the efficiency of perhaps unrivalled social engineering, any lifestyle not serving of this co-operation is marginalised.

The youths I observed to be enjoying their brief freedom from that homogenous, strictly prescribed environment, perhaps to an extent more than is healthy, or even safe. Groups of these playful adolescents spent considerable time lighting fireworks and tossing them here and there on the street outside the hotel. They appeared to pay little attention to where these exploding projectiles were landing, seemingly unconcerned for the potential injury their activity may cause the passer-by or, for that matter, their own companions. The air was charged with an atmosphere of a certain frenzied mania.

What I was witnessing starkly contrasted with the behaviour exhibited within the confines of the Japanese school and work place. Fundamentally at odds with the internalised moral compass of Western Christian socialisation and its abiding feelings of internalised guilt, these institutional systems discipline through the threat of externally imposed shame delivered through the vector of the relevant hierarchy. The flipside of this breeding is the socially irresponsible behaviour of individuals when released from the formalised setting. I had witnessed the behaviour of suited males running amok in late night Tokyo, and of the younger layman on their occasional drunken bouts at the temple. It was all very similar in its reckless abandon, its child-like impulsiveness. The behaviour was tolerated, even expected, the fall out cleaned up as normal scheduled activity resumed.

∞

Thailand is famous for its islands. It has many, over one thousand in total. For the outsider, the islands are perhaps the most common of associations drawn upon mention of the country. I did not spend much time researching before choosing which ones to target. What is the point of contemplating the unfamiliar at length prior to making a decision? Samui was already known to me. It looked beautiful in the photos.

A train, a bus and a ferry delivered me to its threshold. Though when the time came to disembark, I didn't. It felt busy, potentially noisy and distracting, more of a short-term holidaymaker's destination perhaps, and to them I left it. There were still two other islands on the ferry's route. I finished up on the smallest and farthest of this small archipelago, Gaw Dtao, or turtle island. It appeared to be a good choice, quiet, relatively undeveloped, navigable on foot, with a sufficiency of simple bungalow accommodation.

From the port I walked along narrow concrete roadways to the southern coastline and from there followed the beach eastward to the last of the resorts before a headland ended the expanse of white sand. The huts here were well-spaced and spread all the way to the boulders that formed the further shoreline, a drop off point into the beautifully clear emerald water. The place was about half full with international travellers, many of who had already become my junior during my recent period of isolation.

Stewart was one of my neighbours. He was easily identifiable as a Scot through his generous accent, and of an age that exceeded the average backpacker, older even than myself. Although our meeting was brief, it was to become consequential. With an open conversational tone, he quickly defaulted to describing his recent experiences with LSD. After my one experience prior to my departure from Australia, his story was very relatable. I told him of my plan to soon walk the two kilometres to the other side of the island. He asked if I wouldn't mind delivering a tab of LSD on the way, to a friend of his staying in the resort a small way up the beach. I was happy to do so.

By the time of my departure, my plan had attracted the interest of two other parties. Here, as throughout the domain of the international traveller, acquaintances are easily made. A communal atmosphere and the commonality of interest facilitate an absolute ease of socialising. I set off with Australian Simon and German Elena on a route that took us back towards the port, but only a matter of about 500 meters. We ambled and meandered, enjoying the sand, the water and a breeze blowing gently in off the sea. Conversation served to better familiarise to each other's past experience and planned future.

As we approached the neighbouring resort's beachfront restaurant, I could make out the silhouette of a single human form seated at one of the bench tables. I immediately felt whoever it was, they were somehow significant. I could not make out any defining physical features, not even gender, though the feeling was female, slow, smooth, graceful, female. As I approached the open entrance, my eyes confirmed my instincts.

She greeted the three of us with a glance and a smile without troubling to interrupt her activity. Meanwhile I had been halted in my sandy tracks.

I had never before realised such a being existed. During my adolescence there had been girls, girls I had to have, physically attractive girls. Though this female had developed well beyond her inherited beauty, developed in ways adding immeasurably to her appeal.

Her vibrant, yet efficient movement indicated an awareness and intelligence that served her well. She appeared to know herself intimately. Her demeanour felt exquisitely feminine. Its expression presented the perfect foil, harmonious, receptive, yet powerful. I felt she knew me, perhaps not consciously, but in a way that informs her intuition. I felt somewhat naked, transparent, though my attraction to her dwarfed all concern regarding any perceived vulnerability.

Through an exchange of names, we confirmed she was to be the recipient of my delivery. She invited us to sit down. While Elena and Simon sat on the bench opposite, I sat at the next table. I did not wish to involve myself in small talk. Upon this island time is my friend, I clearly felt. There will be opportunity to express myself at a later stage. Sitting at a distance allowed me to continue to exclusively absorb this woman. Sitting any closer would have increased a tension without any practical possibility of imminent auspicious release.

Krista was well-proportioned, curvaceous. Her orange crimped cotton dress draped loosely over her, though not so much as to obscure her figure. Her smooth skin had tanned beautifully under the tropical sun. Her brown hair continued upon a theme, cut short, convenient to the climate. Her almost beak-like nose was perhaps her most unique of physical features, an unusual form, an anomaly accentuating of distinction. Though it was her sensuality that was alluring me. She was quietly oozing it. For her to have moved into sexual activity would not have required a change in mood, simply an increase in intensity. As the uninteresting exchange of words proceeded, I continued to take her in, contented with her probable awareness of my attention.

re-membering

She was occupying herself with the clean-up of a quantity of ganja, removing twigs and seeds, accumulating a considerable pile of separated buds. What followed was an exhibition of honed craft, of service to process, of attention to detail and patient precision. Her slender fingers set about reducing a few selected buds and a touch of added tobacco to crumbs with the aid of scissors of a size appropriate to the long-term itinerant. Her moistened lips enabled the adjoining of rolling papers, within which a fashioned filter of thin rolled cardboard was cupped to form one end of a delicate vessel. Her dexterous hands engaged with sprinkling and spreading the crumbed mix within the curved receptacle, proceeding to iteratively work and shape. With surgical rigour she enclosed the mix, completing a flared flute-like cylinder, bonded through a single slide of her tongue across the protruding edge followed with the caressing seal of her index finger. Tapping and scooping ensued, increasing the already considerable content. A twirling of the tip, and the addition of a small flange provided a rim which self-released when put to the flame in preparation for smoking. I was witnessing an act of love, of devotion, of joy in the activity, and an emerging beauty within the product. She was a master of this craft. The performance enhanced the swelling of my already brimming attraction. I became drawn to her like no one and no thing else existed. All else became a back drop.

Day became night. It was here that all were to stay for the evening. We shared a meal and discussed our plans for tomorrow. Krista expressed interest in joining us on our expedition. She invited us to sleep in her bungalow. We could have just as easily organised our own accommodation, though these arrangements played effortlessly along the lines of my desire.

∞

The island interior remained undeveloped beyond the narrow ill-defined track upon which we found our way. Our destination was another bungalow development, one serviced by canoes equipped with outboard motors connecting it with the island's sole pier situated on the western shore line. This explained the lack of a vehicle-friendly land-based access. Typical of the coastal tropics, coconut palms were abundant and these partially shaded our journey. Large boulders were also plentiful, their presence caused the path to meander and occasionally double-back in order to negotiate small increases in elevation. We took our time, starting out late, and proceeding at a casual pace. Regular pauses provided temporary refuge from the mid-day heat.

We arrived without a hitch by mid-afternoon. The coconut palms made way to a beach mostly rolled flat by the passing of the high tide. To the left, rusty rock flats replaced the sand, receding to a headland of boulders of considerable size. To the right the beach ended in the presence of even larger boulders, weathered and eroded from a mild cliff face constituting the highest point within view. Bungalows spread around us among the palms, all of similar distance from a larger open-sided restaurant situated between them and the ocean at the very rear of the beach where the sand ended and the trees began.

We arranged separate bungalows. The late afternoon was enjoyed through swimming and exploring the rocks bordering the shallow waters. In the evening we sat in the restaurant along with other travellers who had arrived over the days prior. I was seated to Krista's side. The usual banter regarding travel destinations and experiences continued. I did not concern with the conversation; my days of travel were over.

Though I had also as yet done nothing to advance my interest in the woman to which much of my attention was drawn. She began offering glances towards a handsome Frenchman seated opposite. The reaction within me was of panic. I felt a clear call to action. Over the previous four years I had dwelled mostly in the absence of sexual desire and thus equally in the absence of a need for and development of the relevant prowess towards consummation to that end. This now mattered for nothing. I felt I needed to do something immediately.

In a very clumsy manner, I managed to straddle Krista's leg with one of my own. It felt ridiculous. Regardless of how unsophisticated my lunge, it had the desired result. Krista accepted my advance, and soon after we left the restaurant and headed to her bungalow. On the veranda my clumsiness continued, in a struggle to remove her tight leggings. Again, the desired result ensued regardless of my lack of sophistication. I remain deeply in gratitude of this generosity that exists within the heart of new experience, this receptivity to action in the absence of skill.

From here things got a lot easier. Throughout the evening and continuing through the following days and nights we proceeded in mutual, rhythmical, cyclical exploration. She provided a catalyst to return the focus of my attention to within my physicality. I enjoyed the stimulation towards a broader range of emotive experience. She motivated careful reflection in order I detail my thoughts and feelings in the most authentic way. We passed the daylight hours inside the bungalow, emerging in the late afternoon to roam the beach, enjoying the sunset and cool breeze at day's end. We shared the company of others in the restaurant through the evening, though personally, beyond my sexual intimacy within this beautiful tropical land and sea scape, nought else mattered.

I soon found myself a willing collaborator within a shared bubble. It germinated out of immediate attraction, rapidly reducing and encasing us as a translucent sub-field of consciousness. I neither knew nor cared where I ended and she began. I was keenly aware of all her movements, feelings, emotions, the quality of her thoughts, and changes within the aforementioned, all as if my own.

This was an intensity of a kind I had never before experienced. This was a constant responsibility. Now a specific part of what I had become was not within my control. It necessitated total trust. Our union had no place for a past narrative. It was absent of internal self-descriptive projections. It was breathed life through an ongoing serene openness, sensitivity operated non-stop, guided through a synthesis of perspectives, operated through a harmony of movement. It felt unlimited within its limited territory. Potential was explored and manifested creatively through an intuitive free flowing of intelligence from one pole to the other and back. I felt as a ready and joyous participant.

∞

After some weeks we pondered a change of setting and the inevitable stimulation that comes with the journey to new destinations. We moved to the other side of the Thai peninsula, through Krabi, there being the port for a number of islands to the west.

Krista impressed with her flow through the myriad of interactions that followed, negotiating with humour and patience, contributing to joyful experiences for all concerned. We spent much of our time in transit observing fellow travellers and tourists, enjoying the sharing of opinions on the unique acculturated behaviours on show.

We took a boat to Gaw Jum, a comparatively large island, so large that the native community had developed inland areas for rice production, contributing to its diversity of food sources beyond the harvests of its small fishing fleet. It was low season. There were no other travellers at our choice of accommodation. The quietude suited us fine as we continued on our slow harmonious dance through our merged experience.

We developed easy-going relationships with staff, the sole female attended the cooking and cleaning, the several males attended a variety of responsibilities, travelling to Krabi to stock the pantry and to seek out possible new guests, serving in the restaurant and attending to minor maintenance.

Aroon was the oldest of the males, in his 30s. His maturity and confidence allowed for greater interaction and familiarity. What further distinguished him was an economy of meaningful exchange and a more developed sense of what mattered. One evening he invited us to smoke opium at the bungalow he had adopted as his temporary home. Neither Krista nor I had experienced this plant extract before. I was keen to embrace the opportunity, especially being in such an isolated and safe environment.

Our host lay on his side on the mattress that occupied over half of his hut's floor space. We sat on the boards next to him, watching as he prepared the mix. He mashed and added a shredded dry grass to the gooey raw opium in order to render it combustible. After mixing the two substances with a stick, he filled a small cone-shaped receptacle that in turn fit into the entry hose of a ceramic water pipe. I was familiar with the use of such a pipe as a similar technology had been employed in my early days of marijuana use in Australia. Although at that time we fashioned the device from glass bottles within which milk had been delivered to the house, inserting lengths of garden hose, sealing around the hoses inside the bottle's neck with plasticine.

He helped himself to the first pipe, finishing the cone in one. He then repacked the cone before handing it over to me. Following his lead, I attempted to finish it in one breath, although it ended up taking several attempts. The smoke was quite smooth on the throat. The water in the base of the pipe was doing its job.

The effect felt subtle, mild, immediately relaxing. As Aroon began to prepare a pipe for Krista, I began to feel an added sense of conscious expansion. The experience was accompanied by a feeling of increasing euphoria, as if lying in mother's arms, mother nature's arms. Soon my centre began to drift up and out, above the body, hovering within the aerial reaches of the room, and then gently back down again.

I could understand why so many people develop an addiction to this substance or to its various derivatives. For anyone who has this experience, for the time being, nothing in life matters. For those who experience everyday life as troubling, this is a seductive escape. The feeling is so carefree, it wants for nothing. Nothing is preferable.

After imbibing several pipes, we continued to luxuriate in each other's company. It felt as if time had slowed. Exchanges became simple. Aroon introduced descriptions of our activities in the local language. He vocalised his sentences with measured clarity. I repeated his expressions. I knew Thai to be tonal, although my attempts to intonate based upon theoretical conceptions appeared folly. He repeated his sentences patiently. I abandoned technical considerations. Instead I shifted my focus to embracing the feeling of Aroon's pronouncements, as to embody the spirit of the language. It felt as to dwell as the source of the sound was key, and to be its instrument, releasing concern for the end product. From here language tended to more naturally emerge. Resistance disappeared. Vocal cords relaxed. My abandonment had cleared the way. The process became totally impersonal. I disappeared as a formerly describable entity and merged within the midst of the activity. It was as if this was how it felt to be a Thai speaking, carrying with it a way of being, its disposition.

∞

After a week at this resort, a young German couple showed up. They presented with a shyness, both of them similarly withdrawn, reserved, seemingly pre-occupied and distant, sad in similar measure. They expressed an interest in the opium sessions. I got the feeling it would not be the first time for them. I asked Aroon if it was alright if they join us. He did not object, although his response arrived with an air of indifference.

The first time the four of us turned up at his bungalow, we sat on the veranda with Aroon seated upon the threshold of his room. After he had organised a pipe for himself, he again furnished others for myself and Krista. After his second, he again passed me the pipe. I passed it on to the new young couple. Beyond this Aroon provided nothing further. No more pipes were offered, no more free-flowing conversation. The night quickly ended.

After returning to our bungalow, Krista and I engaged in concerned discussion about what had just transpired. Aroon had been not at all hospitable to our new company. I re-called the indifferent tone with which he had delivered his response to my original request for their participation, the way in which those few words now translated within the context of his latter behaviour. This prompted more general reflection on the way in which I conduct myself when gifted exceptional opportunities for rare experience. I was being more and more encouraged to leave more and more alone.

The next day we expressed our sincere gratitude to Aroon for sharing so much of himself with us. We apologised for inviting others to his hosted evenings. We briefly lingered in the silence beyond his evasive response. I examined his facade for any clues to his reasons. No clarification or explanation was forthcoming. Good faith had vanished. The experience was over.

re-membering

∞

As the high season approached, more travellers arrived. The intimacy we shared with the staff further diluted. We started to feel as paying guests. This prompted a change of location. We moved to Phi Phi island where facilities were however more developed and less intimate. This situation lent itself to us spending more time alone together. Meanwhile my visa period was drawing to an end. The time for my departure was drawing closer. As fate would have it, Krista also had an onward ticket to Australia.

One afternoon I awoke from a siesta to find Krista asleep beside me. For the first time since I had first encountered her, I began to ponder my independent future. I did not wish to set foot back within the society of my passed hardships without some sort of plan to support my immunity from regression into old ways.

Amid my rumination, Krista awoke. Without a word, she proceeded to rise from the bed, grab her small bag and exit the bungalow. Hours passed. I finally went in search of her. I walked the length of the beach. She sat at its furthest extremity. The situation was foreboding. I slowed my approach. My awareness heightened. I carefully lowered my body to the sand. I listened.

She questioned my love for her. She accused me of a lack of true commitment. She suggested I never intended for this to be something lasting. She recalled the evening she had called me into the bathroom to witness a small white area within the centre of her menstrual discharge. At that time she explained she had been a month late. Now she was blaming me. I felt there was nothing of value I could say. She was indignant. Perhaps she was right about everything. Though we had never discussed a future together. The practical conclusion was our conclusion. There was no recovering from this. The bubble had burst.

re-membering

activity and activism

My father died after a hellish psychological battle. Years prior he had been diagnosed with Alzheimer's by a member of the medical profession. The condition was first suspected when signs of memory loss emerged resulting in the associated behaviour of general confusion. These symptoms are attributed to the wasting away of brain cells. At the time Alzheimer's was considered a disease for which there is no cure.

My return to the country coincided with the earlier stages of his decline. During my absence he had retired from his previous long-standing managerial responsibilities in the bank. Gone was his identity of institutional authority. His offspring were now all adults of a different generational ethos. Well gone was his role of parental authority. Within the vastness of free time that had opened up for him, beyond his already existing daily church vigilance, he took up some occasional charity work and increased his sporting activity at the local lawn bowling club. None of these activities appeared to provide sufficient sustenance to forestall his decline. The man seemed to no longer have enough sufficiently meaningfully generative engagement to maintain his vitality.

My father's relationship with his wife of over 30 years had always been formal in its presentation. Prayers, chores, pecks on the cheek, all carried out as if someone to be feared was watching in cold judgment. "Yes, mother" he had consistently and immediately reacted. Even through my disinterested adolescent eyes his actions had appeared not heartfelt, much like a going through motions. His matrimonial behaviour combined in a performance of laboured obeisance. There was an absence of visible visceral intimacy, no display of unbridled desire, little heart-felt expression of joy. This façade of the dedicated husband now too began to crack. Uncensored spitefulness occasionally unleashed, his life partner now referred to as the cast-iron lady. All those years of rehearsed homage were now displaying their cost.

Although considered an illness, my direct relationship with my father and his condition did not speak of some discrete physiological cause. The unambiguous indication was one of natural dis-integration. The mainstays of his lifestyle had disappeared, and now too the various internal characterisations assembled for their performance were in decay. In the absence of the preconditions necessary for the maintenance of personas, they are surely undermined. The patterned reactions developed to counter those that represent family, friends, colleagues, clients, being of no further use, fall into disrepair. This reveals the consequence of the obscuring of authentic self-respect and its direct expression. Accumulated resentment is re-sent, in a flood. This plays out in all its social unacceptability.

For the first time in my life it felt immediately useful to share in my father's company. The two of us were simultaneously little attached to the slavish consistency upon which a personality insists. I felt I had already been through the relinquishing of the persona as imposter in its numerous forms.

The crucial difference between my father's experience and mine was that my process was voluntary and conscious. I had sourced and been aided by a lineage of humans that pronounced and embodied a realisation of self more essential than persona. This provided a place of refuge from personality's tyranny. The practice of awareness that had formed the basis of my early meditation years had in turn witnessed many and varied facades in their coming and going. This witnessing inherently provided insight, as that which can be sighted is thus revealed as not forming a necessary part of that which is sighting.

The culture of my parent's generation, and most poignantly, its church, is silent on such knowledge. Left alone without device at a time of most need, my father faced terror amid personal disintegration. The contemporary church appeared to only suture the existential concerns of its adherents in life, doing little to effectively prepare them for death. Mention of the subject is generally avoided, or treated through the application of myth as a means of temporary relief from the discomfort of consideration.

This is a curious situation considering death's eternal proximity, its ultimate unavoidability, suggested finality and the attendant implications. My only conclusion can be the church does not exist for its flock. Rather it functions as all organs, organisms and organisations, in a symbiotic alliance of self-perpetuity. It is an unholy relationship as it does not attend to the whole. It does not actually attend to all matters of life and death to which it purports.

The medical profession's response is equally revealing in its blindsiding of death. In diagnosing my father's process as an illness, it insinuates therefore the condition is not a natural part of life's passing. My father's vitriolic outbursts conveniently avoided scrutiny by being announced as the utterances of someone not well. Attempts at placation insisted the words and actions of dementia were in no sense meaningful.

re-membering

The broad cultural attitude not only displays as a symptom of a community desperately determined to avoid any talk of the conditions approaching life's end, it as much misses an opportunity to fundamentally cleanse society of so much deceit, and the personal ill-health that remains its consequence.

An associated lesson is missed here regarding the cost of insincere communications within intimate relationships. If my father's antics and utterances had been respected as the consequences of suppressed genuine feelings, then this knowledge may immediately and directly feed back into comprehensive community reflection on what constitutes true relationship. To avoid the uncomfortable discussion is to deprive future generations of so much opportunity for authentic emotional expression and outlet, whispered musings, light-heartedness, dance, games, intimacy, touch, caress, sexual exploration; its honesty disclosing learning, easing development, fulfilment, love, wisdom, empowerment, resolution, letting go, moving on, renewal, ….

I suspect the unconscious aim of all left unaddressed is to ease disturbance on the utility of a system that worships the material, at the expense of acknowledgement of the non-material. Within this the vast majority colludes. If it's not matter, it doesn't matter, it's immaterial.

The usual dose of heavy sedatives was administered to my father. This temporarily debilitated the man, and in so doing relieved those closest of much of his much-misunderstood challenging assaults.

∞

During the ritual of my father's funeral, the same telling social priorities manifested themselves like some elaborate dark conspiracy. Attendees at such gatherings know well of what is expected of them. Words of praise attempt to paint the deceased in terms of unique upstanding quality. Tears are shed as the subject of death rears its head, perhaps in reaction to the fear this inspires, or in lamentation of the vacancy the departed has left for many, or as a show of personal virtue. Non-engagement in the solemn theatre may lead to the offender's out casting, even excommunication, too high a price for such social organisms.

These social patterns persist within the same cultural environment as the belief in a heavenly destination awaiting the virtuous beyond death. This belief suggests the appropriate setting for someone's passing should be celebratory, not sorrowful.

Perhaps funerals are less about the deceased and more about those that remain. Even though the church warns against such selfish concern as of moral impropriety, it still colludes in setting the maudlin scene. To suggest the whole state of affairs as a contradiction, or further, a hypocrisy, is likely to be met with offence. Though the taking of offence, as always, only serves to indicate the existence of some deeper level of neglect or insincerity.

An honest rendering of what the occasion of death represents may serve the living in powerful and loving purpose. It invites all to take pause and reflect in order to reorder priorities in alignment with what is truly important in life. It motivates people to live more for the day, eschew indifference, and make the most of opportunities. The impact of such behaviour is undoubtedly powerfully cathartic. Who knows the potential that this represents for both the individual and the collective?

In examining recorded history alone, it would be quite reasonable to conclude humanity never broadly and consistently embodied a culture that contained the tools and traditions, and most importantly the seers, to ensure self-knowledge of sufficient depth informed all matters of life and death. The threads of development commonly traced into the past raise consistent themes of warfare, persecution and control. This places doubt between the lines, as depicted regimes of such dictatorial dominance necessarily insist upon censor, banish utterance of contrary culture, belief and practice. This frames written history as a narrative convenient to the reigning power elites, representing a thin slither of doctrine amid all else that failed to triumph through the past's bloody battles, all this set within temporal limit, within the 5 000 years of written script.

This scenario opens the imagination to so much more of what may have passed unrecorded through the planet's considerable human past. All manner of knowledgeable societies may have existed. There is considerable circumstantial evidence of this turned up in archaeological finds and more directly within the remnants of long surviving tribal societies that sufficiently escaped the torments of the empires from within which written history emerged.

There is sufficient respect and sympathy expressed in honouring how my father truly lived. The man appeared to labour under trying circumstances. He was born amid the mindsets of the depression and world war generation, moulded in earnest, disciplined to a life pursuant of material security and religious piety. He was corralled into compliance without reasonable social alternative. Direct pathways to the divine, to truth, to knowledge were condemned, tantamount to blasphemy. Without sufficient mentoring in the nurturing of the soul, he busied himself within the buttressing of his impermanent life through toil and unquestioned belief.

re-membering

∞

My return to Australia also coincided with the peak of my brothers' musical success. Immediately after touching down I was to witness their impressive performance in support of a pair of the country's most prominent rock bands.

In my regular early attendance of further shows I was motivated through a desire to dance. It came as naturally as an infant's will to walk. It was as if my years of temple life had not only heightened my sensitivity through its spartan lifestyle, it had also removed earlier conditioned barriers to acting on impulse. This was now celebrating an inflow of stimulus.

My movement was effortless, bathing in the sonic ocean that I had first experienced years ago through the agency of marijuana, although now without such ally. The practically unlimited points of attention within the sounds generated inspired equally unlimited ways of rhythmically creative body motion. The dance floor felt to be the best place in the house, right next to the band and speakers, with a smooth floor surface that facilitated navigation without the need for visual guidance.

My ease of conspicuous activity usually encouraged others to join. I created no such images regarding who these people may be. They could have been anyone or no one, and they were. It was not important. Important was only the outflow of harmonious movement and the simultaneous inflow of musical activity that inspired its innovation.

Australians had become quite an alien bunch in my absence, to the extent it would not be entirely accurate to report the experience as a feeling of return. The feeling was of being here for the first time, simultaneously infused with a sense of ethereal familiarity. This was not quite as a culture shock; I retained a visceral memory of how to move within this milieu.

Yet I lacked the conviction of a well-rehearsed narrative, as if to find myself in a play without having read the script. People treated me as if one of them, and I engaged, somewhat short on character. The circumstances remained unthreatening however. Everything arose as if in slow motion, events as if less frequently happening, the speech of the citizenry as if drawn out. Voluminous space enveloped all.

The culture had morphed, albeit through the change that shows up between one generation and the next. I was a stranger to the emerging feminist zeitgeist most evidently exhibited in the manner of the young urban tertiary educated women and men.

Perhaps due to the preceding reputation of my recent exotic experiences and my felt freedom from the invisible constraints of endemic culture, I attracted the interest of a number of these females. I had no ideas of how to proceed.

My recently rediscovered limitlessness of being was now my baseline experience, and thus lacked anything prescriptive with which to inform sexual manoeuvrings within this novel atmosphere. I felt as an ancient infant. I did not feel the female's overt displays of confidence tolerable of unbridled expressions of raw masculinity. Accordingly, I displayed interest, though responded naively. The girls took the lead. In the bedroom things felt somewhat rudderless.

In retrospect, honest discussion would have perhaps helped. At the time the situation was not of significant concern, although duly noted. I had returned to society with a focus on the community. Specifically, this did not include the fulfilment of sensual desire as a going concern. The implications of this were to emerge by degrees.

∞

Griffith University provided a Science Degree advertised to arm students with the skills to help meet the environmental challenges of the coming century. There appeared to be some truth to this claim evidenced in the diversity of subjects available.

Courses provided an introduction to the study of rocks, soils, water, living things and their respective chemical compositions and inter-relationships; the study of societal, administrative, legal and political institutions to be engaged to facilitate favourable environmental outcomes within the context of developmental planning and projects; and the research methods, statistics and mathematics necessarily employed to draw meaningful conclusions regarding all of the aforementioned. I enrolled.

My activist life on campus started briskly. Many of the main players were to be my fellow first year students. Organisings were underway for the hosting of a national students' conference for sustainability. In an enthusiasm to maximise my utility, I volunteered to manage the finances, not only for the conference but also for the club that was formed for the purpose of making it happen.

The preparations brought together a disparate group of both school leaving and mature age students, ranging from those with a passion for the natural environment, those concerned about pollution and energy inefficiency, individuals motivated to develop sustainable lifestyles, groups that prioritised gender and racial equality, those with an interest in politics or the management of the economy, and outdoor activity enthusiasts.

These different groups combined to present a diverse social dynamic in and around the hub that became my social life. Alliances sprung up among interests in common, but as much contributed to factions around areas of ideological dissonance. Values presented often failed to provide sufficient grounds for uniform co-operation and community.

Upon recognition of the diversity of perspectives present, I focused on the maintenance of overall social cohesion, feeling unity as paramount if we were at all to succeed in influencing the lifestyle choices of the greater population beyond academia. To this end, I tended to leave the extraneous assertions of others unchallenged.

I'm not sure about the virtue of this policy. Remaining silent perhaps may result in a perceived association with a mistaken idealism by omission, and probably has consequences. Though I'm not sure speaking up would have made much difference either, knowing the poor history of attempting to offer unsolicited differing perspectives. People become defensive. Discussion becomes divisive. Such conversations would have required personally unprecedented appeals for love and wisdom. Though certainly this would have aided my social and emotional development.

Through my supporting of the management structures of a number of clubs and societies, I had begun to associate with a significant number of women who were active within the politics of the feminist movement. I recall their stated opposition to their gender's sexual objectification as inherently confusing. Is not the experience of attraction inspired through the imagination? And in imagination what is not objectified? Is not all meaning nurtured in this manner? Is not such objection on the part of these females grounded itself in an objectification, that which interprets male behaviour convenient to personal competitive advantage?

What sort of worldly behaviour may be uniquely set apart and accused of objectification? Of course, instances of abuse are not acceptable, though as such, are already legislated, policed and litigated against within the current system. Further, abuse may flow either way, between or within genders, within any sphere of social life.

This politicised anti-objectification stance potentially affects the essential flow of courtship and mating behaviour. It felt to introduce a confusion, to throw into doubt assured physical instigation, shifting emphasis towards the clear prior consent of the female. I couldn't see the ancient dance ever succumbing to attempts at such domestication. It appeared as if to surrender an intuitive art to the regimens of intolerable formality. If popularised, such a stand appeared a major concern for individuals of a sexually reproducing species just recently emancipated from the shackles of past generational oversight.

Again, the theme of sex and sexuality had reared its head, this time within the sphere of gender diplomacy. Again, I chose to remain silent of my musings, and within the sphere of my activism, I determined to remain pragmatically celibate.

Elsewhere personal doubts arose through my involvement within the environmental movement more broadly. I occasionally involved myself in direct actions on and off campus. One such event had been organised as to draw attention to a structural development progressing close to a waterway within the university grounds. There I stood within a body of students across the entrance to the site, attempting to prevent the movement of large vehicles in and out. Beyond any concern regarding personal safety, the experience questioned my grounds for involvement.

I knew very little of practical detail regarding what constituted sustainable, environmentally sensitive development. Specifically, I had no inkling of the process that had been undertaken in order for this development to go ahead. Perhaps all possible research, studies, technologies, and precautions had been taken into consideration and implemented. My involvement rested on a good faith partnering with those who organised the protest. This no longer sat well with me. It made clear the requirement for much prior learning and information-gathering in order to operate in alignment with my values, and much skill development in order to be effective in my contribution. These matters are extremely complex. This would need to be a full time, long term occupation.

∞

As the time for the conference grew closer, voluntary assistance became less and less conspicuous. I took on more and more responsibility. This included providing greater support to the paid co-ordinator, helping to structure the conference programme and liaise with presenters, corresponding with relevant officials, attending meetings, organising volunteers and equipment, assisting in grant application correspondence, continuing to manage finances, whatever was needed to keep things on track towards the quickly approaching deadline.

re-membering

On the morning of the start of the conference I arrived at the main lecture theatre for the official opening. Typically, separate small groups of attendees lingered around the outside of the entrance doors. Off to the side I caught sight of the conference co-ordinator with whom I had worked with closely over a period of months.

She stood alone, tears running down her face. She was despairing of the lack of organisation and the personnel to carry it off. She pointed out the vice-chancellor of the university and the professor who was to deliver the morning's keynote address standing unattended. The president of the club formed in order to facilitate the conference's execution was nowhere to be seen. I felt simultaneously the dread of proceeding to take the lead and the firming of my sense of responsibility to do just that.

I walked away from the hesitation that would have prolonged my suffering, gathered a pen and paper and made notes regarding all that I could think of that required attention. I then split up these listed items into separate duties a number of those present may fulfil. Next, I approached three students with which to explain the plan. They all agreed to their suggested roles. I then approached the vice-chancellor and professor and ushered them down to the front of the lecture theatre. I approached the dais, stood behind it and waited for the best moment to begin addressing the crowd that by now had mostly taken seats. Other-worldly calm descended within my being, though with a spirit tending towards flight. I felt a need to remain grounded, though without distracting too much from the words that required gathering and delivery in a tone sufficiently warmly welcoming for strangers to this place and occasion.

I managed my performance in a way that got the job done, although with some distance from fluency and completeness. I handed over to another student who was to explain more specific details. I walked off the stage, up the carpeted stairs, sliding into a chair close to the conference co-ordinator. She inquired of my well-being. I replied with barely containable glee. My adequate performance of the impromptu task had greatly enhanced my outlook on what was personally achievable. I sat there feeling there was nothing I could not do.

As the conference rolled on, I busied myself with the logistics of scheduled events. Without immediate involvement in specific sessions, I could only really observe in glimpses. Individuals from my own campus, inconspicuous in the organising, now emerged as conspicuous consumers of the presentations on offer. Delegates from other universities throughout the country were also present in considerable numbers due to the subsidy of their home institutions.

I recall paying a visit to an address from the lord mayor of the city. This man had facilitated many environmental initiatives during his time in office. He innovated the development of green corridors and connecting bicycle paths throughout the city, car-pooling on major freeways, and recycling bins for every household. Regardless, this man was criticised and attacked by members of the predominantly student audience. I guess this was happening because he represented government, and thus targeted as the enemy.

I further re-call arranging a night of music and socialising for all participants to enjoy and get to know each other. Many interstate delegates did not attend, instead deciding to go off into the city and partake in fast food at the world's largest of chain restaurants.

After the conference had ended, my responsibilities continued in the settling of finances. We had ended the conference in financial surplus due to the granting of monies and profits from social events. The surplus money created unforeseen problems and thus personal challenges. As treasurer and finance coordinator I was caught up in a feud on what to do with the surplus. One faction wished to share it as payment among those who contributed to the success of the conference. Another faction insisted that we had worked as volunteers and thus we should proceed in this spirit, donating the funds to the organisers of next year's event. There was also much tension and debate regarding who should take responsibility for the compilation of the proceedings to be published and distributed throughout the nation's library system.

My experiences during the conference were rich, though as much due to their revelations of prevailing behaviours appearing to undermine the advancement of formalised goals. On show were notable examples of dis-interest in productive co-operative contribution from those who directly benefited. Preparations and events revealed key individuals absent when most needed. I repeatedly witnessed displays of archaic tribal behavioural tendencies. It appeared many participants took the opportunity to their own narrow advantage, seeking shelter and meaning among those of similar identification, self-proclaiming as virtuous, and antagonising of outsiders. Such behaviour provided a limiting sense of self-worth for individuals who at the same time commonly continued to imbibe of their youthful indulgences in contradiction of their stated values.

I hadn't given the sustainability cause much detailed consideration before or since my involvement began. I, perhaps like many, originally found motivation as a concerned member of a humanity rapacious in its destruction of its own life-supporting ecology through a blinding cultural preponderance with material acquisition. The situation had been momentous enough to feel keenly of a need to do something to assist in a community education towards an understanding of this trajectory.

Though after exposure to the conference culture, it became apparent exclusive identity politics and self-centred acquisitive behaviour remained a common feature of its participants. Absent was a recognition of the depth of this problem. Surely the level of integrated co-operation necessary for a globally sustainable humanity could only proceed from a core community aware and acknowledged of their own primal and socialised motivations and the inherent counter-productive consequences of them. At a bare minimum, only a group diligently inclusive and wary of their personal attachments could address and counter the ancient tendency to oppose and sabotage that perceived as of other, and in the process provide a foundational example for a more inclusive, less destructive mode of operation within broader society.

My summary experiences led to a careful re-consideration on the question of sustainability. If life is accepted as something taking place on a planet where all is subject to the ravages of slow degradation and periodic cataclysm, it must be accepted that life here will come to an end eventually, the same may be stated for the fate of the planet itself. As is for individual life, the environment equally cannot be saved, neither the world.

In terms of relative life choices, the situation is complex. Humans not only continue to require resources to survive, they continually desire resources sufficient to thrive. In addition, those that struggle are not in a position to concern with environmental health. They will do whatever they feel necessary in order to survive the day. Thus, there are no solutions to environmental issues, only on-going management strategies. It became clear the decision to live in a way that supports a robust sustainability is a lifestyle choice. Personally, I felt I had graduated out of activism.

Emotionally, a major side-effect of the conference adventure was burn out. Prior to the experience I didn't realise such a condition even existed. Symptoms began as painful feelings of debilitation in reaction to any arising idea suggestive of required effort. Intuitively, it felt as if my energy stores had run dry. It was as if I had nothing left to give. The symptoms were re-minding of existence as comprised of and reliant upon a limiting accumulation of essential energy.

Like my depression as an adolescent, this condition led to the suspension of all activity beyond that immediately necessary in the servicing of my pre-existing commitments. It was insisting upon my rest and reflection. Though this time, in contrast to my period of depression, the problem related to my mode of operation, not to an absence of meaningful activity. Specifically, my state promoted a questioning of my degree of personal involvement in my worldly engagements. Since my return to the country I had increasingly re-engaged in an unguarded extraneous striving at the expense of this source of vitality, in neglect of what I had realised through years of awareness training.

Going forward I determined to continue engaging inspiration, though within the context of an effortless flow, leaving behind the mis-guided energy over-investment referred to and often promoted as selflessness.

∞

All the while, my academic studies proceeded. They began with enthusiasm and slowly waned by degrees. This is reflected in my results, starting with high distinctions in first year, and ending with not much better than passes in the final year.

The degree was structured in such a way that revised school science in first year and thus took nothing for granted in terms of what new students already knew. It then introduced the diversity of areas of potential specialisation in second year, before in the final year further detailed an area of specialisation chosen by the student. In terms of a further though connected required choice, my major shifted from policy studies, through planning, to ecology, reflecting a shift from the area first thought to be the most important in terms of effecting societal change to the area of most appeal personally, being that of the natural world.

Policy studies were tedious. Further demotivation lay with the uncertainty surrounding policy's efficacy in bringing about desirable long-term outcomes. Historically, policy appeared to shift back and forth, left and right. Legislation remains vulnerable to amendment or repeal. I was becoming increasingly aware the challenges facing humanity regarding the potential for any such healthily sustainable relationship within the natural world hinged upon issues more fundamental than political decision-making. All problems appeared to emanate from the very way relationship with nature is culturally perceived.

Science is commonly seen as a collection of facts about us, the world and the universe. It is actually a method for the establishing of theories through evidence. Facts can change. They almost all do, given enough time. Scientific research methods require assumptions, for example, that nature is orderly, and that everything has a cause. Science relies upon probability in order to establish findings. In other words, if a specific outcome of an experiment happens 95% of the time it might be accepted as proof. Individual research projects require a review of all relevant previous literature in order that conclusions do not contradict what has already been established without strong supporting evidence. All these considerations make for a discipline assuming in its statements, uncertain in its findings, and limited by its precedent.

A fundamental assumption of science has been that there exists a world of matter and energy outside ourselves, that this world exists the same for all, and thus is able to be understood objectively. This assumption has been rigorously challenged and investigated over the past century.

By now the well-known 'double-slit experiment' has become the corner stone of an area of research that has given rise to a contrary view in the field of quantum physics. To summarise the findings of the original study, when sub-atomic particles were shot at two slits within a barrier, they ended up creating a pattern on a screen placed on the other side of the barrier consistent with the behaviour of spread out waves. When observed through a measuring device the particles created two simple bands on the screen, with each particle only passing through one of the slits, suggesting they acted as discrete objects. The conclusion drawn was that the act of observing caused the wave to 'collapse' and bring about the existence of matter.

It has since been claimed the act of observation not only determines existence and location, it also effects behaviour or properties, and not only of electrons, but also of larger objects. Further, exhibited properties appear inconsistent. Electrons may exhibit certain properties when originally measured, and then exhibit different, even opposite properties when measured at a later time. As a result, the term 'super-position' was coined to describe the nature of electrons prior to any specific measurement. Humanity did not previously have a term for something that could be this, that, both or neither, in other words, for something that subsists as potential.

The conclusion arising from this body of research is there is simply no objective reality. There is only the experience of matter, or any experience, when we are observing, and when we do so, we have significant influence over the nature of the experience. Without our observation, nothing of discrete property exists, neither space nor time, everything is merely potential within an open field of energy. This implies that no external realm for a god exists either, that any notional god can only be instrumental through us, for we are the ones that bring about space and time through our observations. This not only means science can no longer maintain its claim of objectivity, but more importantly, it has significantly pointed to the inseparably intimate nature of divinity.

This elegant explanation of events not only coincides with my own ongoing direct experiences, it also accounts for the otherwise seemingly contradictory behaviour of different human populations. Inhabiting the same planet are communities that believe in ghosts, that believe in nature spirits, that believe in magic, that may be viewed as superstitious by others. Groups of humans may believe in a single god, in multiple gods, may not believe in a god. There are those that believe in empirical facts. There are those that believe in a range of contrasting perspectives, and those who may not believe in anything. A single modern-day individual may believe in ghosts, luck, pray to a god, practice science, and support equality among people of different identity, beliefs and perspectives. This rich diversity of worldly experience suggests an interface that indeed relies pivotally on the role of the experiencer, that the very exercise of experiencing is participatory, and that an array of potential remains at the ready to accommodate manifold world views.

Quantum mechanical findings demonstrate the detached distance required between subject and object in order to reveal the essential nature of the relationship. Within the methods of reductionism, it appears this distance is not met, resulting in propositions of a consistent human-centrism.

Humans brought up within the common scientific cultural paradigm are educated to believe we exist at the top of a food chain, we are the most clever of species, the world is otherwise ostensibly devoid of intelligence, and it is thus up to us to manage nature within this circumstance. Through the widespread currency of these ideas, modern society perpetuates a narrow band of perceptions convenient in justifying the elevation of its own importance. We are infatuated with these projections without knowing them as projections.

This subconscious mis-taking of the fruits of personal perspective for an objective reality not only leaves us dis-placed, in no position to wholly comprehend what stands directly before us, it renders us dis-oriented, directionally opposed to the possibility of revealing our inextricably intimate implication in the character of its appearance. This ignorance promotes our illusory alienation, and maintains our dissociation from essential wisdom. We deprive ourselves of the universal knowledge present prior to the incisive dis-integrating effect of perception, of that which abides within consciousness itself.

Beyond the many direct painful consequences of conclusions drawn and actions taken based upon such discriminating human-centric scrutiny are the knock-on effects, the potential for on-going unintended, often accumulative or exponential, destructive repercussions through so many means.

The assumptions that underpin scientific theory serve the same utility as religious belief. They are accepted as a basis for worldly assertion without or in willed ignorance of knowledge. Scientists have argued with vehement fervour equal to that of clergy that science is based upon evidence. Though scientific assumptions are not truths, and when challenged, evidence may be conveniently re-interpreted, or simply ignored.

Another similarity between science and religion arises out of their general ideological exclusivity. This sets respective adherents in conflict, even though it is just as easy to imagine a world where evolutionary processes interact harmoniously within the creation of a solitary god, and even though it is also possible to imagine a belief in a solitary god emerging through the evolution of a long succession of human belief systems, that is, through natural process of selection.

The presence of conflicts among ideologues of differing belief systems points to a history of adversity not limited to the often tension between religion and science. It appears we don't fight due to the especially convincing nature of our convictions; we fight because differing perspectives appear to threaten destruction of our limiting vision of a world, a vision upon which we feel our lives depend. This is no less because the ideologies invocative of our world view are inherited complete with a guarantee of unique authenticity. Thus, founding principles normally remain unexamined as to their nature, and thus we too remain unexamined as to ours.

Though we are conscious. We have the capacity to be aware of what is true and not true, even in the absence of understanding and explanation. The direct insight which is exactly awareness allows for all to be seen relative to and in the context of the absolute. This is the radically free mind. What is hence beholden is without bias and thus requires no defensive argument nor bloodshed.

∞

I was no longer interested to be an activist or a scientist. My experience was indicating that choice births ends rather than means. An activist, rather than saving the world, perpetuates a world in need of saving, as a scientist develops and perpetuates theoretical perspectives in concession to pet preconceptions and future aspirations.

I turned my heart's gaze to lifestyle. I began to dream of being on the land. I yearned to enjoy an intimacy within this timeless continent. At the same time, I wished to nurture my self. Within nature I could establish a home base and invite others to join, share the experience, and nurture mutually.

the ancient continent and her unfamiliar inhabitants

The call came out of nowhere. I hadn't heard from Mark since our brief reunion immediately following my arrival from the Orient. That meeting was now already two years passed, though I remember it well.

There I stood in the house of my adolescence with an old friend who had accompanied so many of my first experiences in unfettered freedom. He was relating with familiarity. I was no longer that guy. I never was. It was a role I had played in those circumstances. Those circumstances were no more. It was like being mistaken for someone that I once knew, like that person was being summoned. It was challenging not to succumb. It was an uncomfortable encounter. Suffice to say, I did not contribute much to that conventional play of nostalgia, neither did I explain much in terms of my present. I did not know where to begin regarding the latter. My contemporary realisations had as yet insufficient cultural context. I felt as a foreign guest, and so reserved my activity.

And now this call from the void. It reached me as I was holidaying within montane hinterland just over an hour's drive north of Brisbane, at a house left in the minding hands of university friends. It would have taken him some searching to locate my whereabouts.

He explained with enthusiasm regarding a job on offer. A camp facility under construction on the shore of Moogerah Dam required a manager. The Catholic Church had purchased land and hatched the project, made possible due to the bequest of a recently-deceased former parishioner of that region.

This opportunity came my way through the agency of a former classmate who had ordained into the church. Father Paul had developed quite a network within the local organisation, becoming privy to many of its activities. He was on good terms with the priest within the parish where the camp was now under construction. I relayed my enthusiasm for the position and agreed to a meeting at the site.

∞

The ground is so hard in this area that at least a crow bar would be required to make a hole within which to plant a tree. Even then, if an appropriately tough species is not chosen, the tree, at best, would only develop within the limits of the hole dug for it. This is the territory of the ironbark. This common name was appropriately chosen, beyond reference to the hardness of the wood, it infers the degree of strength required to penetrate the soil within which the roots need to expand. The canopy of this former woodland provides insufficient shade to protect sensitive skin from burning under the sharp sun. Leaves provide a mere dappling relief upon the earth below. Ground cover is sparse, top soil is equally sparse, exposing a clayish subsoil that expands on the rare occasion of rain, and contracts and cracks in harmony with the moisture's rapid evaporation.

The Australian continent as a whole is ancient. It is said to possess the oldest rocks on the planet. The top soils parented through the eras have since substantially been eroded and long washed away. Minimal tectonic activity has provided limited new rock material from the earth's depths. The little soil generated from new rock does not maintain replacement rates. Twenty percent of the continent is classified as desert and five percent suitable for cropping, fertility declining significantly by the year. This reality contests reference to the golden soil celebrated and immortalised in the national anthem of this land's newest nation.

The wide-spread lack of soil nutrient is reflected in the makeup of endemic animal populations. Reptiles, insects and birds abound, larger mammals almost completely absent. Snakes and lizards survive aided by their efficiency of movement and ability to absorb energy directly from the Sun. Many insects maintain as an integral part of their strategy an ability to lay dormant within the soil during times of insufficient rainfall. Birds of many species conveniently migrate, at times even pre-empting the coming of regional abundance elsewhere. The absence of large native mammals with their large energy requirements may be similarly accounted for by the land's lack.

In recent years the continent has become internationally notorious for its bush fires, almost entirely interpreted through a tragedy narrative of human death and property destruction. Ecological perspective yields a less catastrophic interpretation, more a story of adaptation, utility and necessity. Many dry land plant species aid their fire survival with thick bark armour or an ability for post-fire coppice growth. Elsewhere fire provides an essential role in seed pod activation. In other parts of the world large grazing herds recycle grassland vegetation, providing nutrients for a diversity of life forms through their excretions. On this continent, in the relative absence of grazing animals, it is the fires that make nutrients available in the form of ash. The conflagrations are viewed with little acknowledgment of this essential role they play in nature's recycling.

There is often complaint of drought among the country's rural inhabitants. Their words may well express more a yearning for rainfall sufficient to quench the needs of their exotic crops and livestock, rather than an accurate measure of current rainfall relative to past averages. Australians of colonial and post-colonial foreign descent almost exclusively eat species of plants and animals introduced to the continent since colonial times. Beyond ocean harvests, the only commonly notable exception to this is the macadamia nut. Kangaroos outnumber people approximately two to one on the continent, though are rarely consumed.

In their demand for and farming of produce not practically evolved in and thus unsuited to local conditions, the human inhabitants further contribute evidence of a population significantly ignorant of, and consequentially mal-aligned with, their newly adopted habitat.

∞

As the meeting proceeded it became clear there was little competition for the position. It appeared the main obstacle to my chances was the idea a husband and wife team would be preferred. The site was isolated and so considered best suited for a couple to share company and the many responsibilities. Essential to the job was the provision of meals and day time activities to sizeable groups, on top of keeping the place maintained, clean and developing. I obviously showed enough to convince Paul that I was adequately able to fulfil all responsibilities without the need for a partner.

At the start of my post the camp remained in a state of incompletion. I had no residence. The house was yet to be re-situated from a nearby township where it had stood for generations. For months I slept in one of the huts newly constructed to house guests.

The committee set up to manage the camp was selected of men with no experience in camp management. I also had no experience, though I had a vision of what I wanted to create. I had a will to make the place the best facility of its type in the region.

There were already many camps, including three pre-existing on the shores of Moogerah Dam. The market was saturated. Many schools had their own facilities providing outdoor education to their students in its various forms. These camps were subsidised by the schools, so economic viability was not of priority concern to them. As a consequence, we could always be undercut on price. My opportunity lay in customer satisfaction. To my advantage, the reputation of many existing facilities was not positive. Often run by ex-army personnel with a background in discipline, other camps regularly lacked the kind of staff able to provide fun and fulfilling experiences to children.

I set about the considerable task of developing quality services with minimal rules, aiming to relax, engage and educate. Of course, this was going to take time. In the beginning my priority was to simply help guests feel comfortable. This mainly required information so that group leaders could manage their charges in a way that optimised safety, peace of mind, and positive experience. Guest responsibilities, specifically self-service and cleaning, were designed to minimise my involvement. Water supply remained a concern, specifically ensuring urban youths co-operated in conserving this essential resource. Drinking water was solely sourced from the sky.

During periods of guest occupancy my greatest challenge were the meals, targeted to be tasty, filling, nutritious, punctual, while at scale and within budget. This was a business in itself. No corners could afford to be cut. Meals needed to contribute to the comfort and health of young children away from home, and to not provide any reason for negative news communicated back to parents.

Early results were inconsistent. I recall a group of 100 senior girls having to wait 2 hours for dinner one evening. The problem was a lack of familiarity with the second-hand commercial oven which leaked heat from its base. This group never returned.

My friend-suggested, consciously-adopted attitude of having nothing to lose in taking the job served me well at times like this. I accepted such mishaps as a necessary part of the process of skill development, and skill development as a necessary part of the realisation of dreams.

∞

The early months were spent mostly alone. The camp was situated along a dirt road that ended at the dam's shoreline, so there wasn't much passing traffic either. I spent so much time in the absence of human company that trains of thought began to fall apart. This phenomenon suggests the existence of thoughts to be reliant upon verbal exchange, outlets into the world, for their continued integrity. This presents thoughts and words as of a seamless relation. In the absence of company, thoughts are not getting a chance to be aired and reinforced through conversation, and thus begin to fragment. The not so uncommon instances of children apparently conversing with imaginary friends, and of people more broadly conversing with spirits or talking to themselves, all reflect the importance of this relationship between thoughts and words. Although not presenting a challenge of consequence for my health, I remained keen to find a solution to my lack of a social life.

Boonah, the nearest town of size, though situated just to the other side of a small mountain range to the east, required a 25 km circuitous drive. I began to visit a pub at the edge of this town on Friday evenings. The place was very lively on these occasions, complete with band and a rowdy crowd that filled the lounge, public bar and veranda. I was immediately set upon from among the comparatively small numbers of girls. Their eyes glared ravenous. I also drew much attention from the guys, though their eyes glared with menace.

Perhaps fortunately, the owners of the pub were new comers from Sydney. The sons shared more of my earlier cultural background. I quickly became friends with the younger of the two. Terry enjoyed DJing and was popular with a number of the local girls. Our alliance made it possible to socialise away from the daunting atmosphere of the pub. I would often visit Terry in his comfortable A-frame abode, beautifully situated on a small rise at the base of the low mountains.

Rural society remained clearly traditional. I imagined interactions with the local females would be less complicated than as with their evolving urban sisters. Here, men were men and women were women, with little in between, I thought. Typically, I was not prepared for the reality. The girls I met were no strangers to fist fighting, nor to taking powerful cars through their stunts. In their natural habitat they stood unabashed and loud. I had not been previously exposed to such an assault.

re-membering

At times I felt of insufficient physical and emotional strength to stand up to the challenge the rural community posed. Within me, what previously postured as an ethic of non-violence was now, at least in significant part, exposed as cowardice in disguise. This revealed the downside of a well-intended protected upbringing.

I was not going to give up however. It was I who sought for this uninhibited breath of fresh air, this broader social mobility. It was I who sought and welcomed less social complexity and the potential value it may offer. The companionship of one of the more relatable local girls appeared as a manageable interim compromise. Julie felt less unnerving, perhaps due to her semi-urban upbringing. Though still she regularly danced on tables, flashed her tits at unsuspecting male strangers, swore to effect and pissed outdoors when and wherever she felt the need.

I took up touch football as a further avenue to social opportunity. As much as this sport relies on team work, many of my team did what they could to avoid me on and off the field. Even when I played an outstanding game, nothing was mentioned. I had already experienced a level of racism first hand during my time in Japan, though in this part of rural Australia I was of the same race as the local community. This was more of a class issue. However it may be branded, it looked of a broader group of behaviours that in common sort to identify difference in order to avoid the threat of impact on the comfortably familiar.

I did not take it personally. I knew it could and would happen to any new comer. They did not know who I was. Neither did it cause much inconvenience. It did not deprive me of any desired experience. On the contrary, if I had been accepted unconditionally it would have meant more social responsibility, spending more time with people who I was beginning to see shared little in common in terms of aspiration nor lifestyle. Regardless, it remained fascinating that people who lived so close to the city could be so different.

∞

Catholic schools were the camp's sole source of clients for some time. Twelve schools had formed an association contributing funds to the facility's development in exchange for occupancy at discount rates. A significant number of these schools came with expectations of service beyond what I had agreed to provide. The employment contract stated I was to manage the facility in return for a wage, and that any activities or meals provided could be privately negotiated and compensated. These associated schools were often not happy with having to pay extra for activities. I was not agreeable to providing free activities which would have meant more work beyond what was already a busy schedule. Ironically, most of these schools for which the camp had been built quickly ceased using it.

The local country Catholic schools avoided the facility due to grievances regarding the very choice of building the project. The deceased man's estate stipulated his bequeathed resources be used to benefit the community. This was interpreted by the church's administrators as to provide a resource for the benefit of the community at large. The local parishioners were angered as they felt they should have been more directly advantaged.

∞

I continued to work on my social life. I had recognised this to be the key to my longer-term survival. A casual relationship with Julie developed, although interestingly, she admitted to sleeping around, motivated by an insecurity regarding my longer-term loyalty. I had previously never thought this a possible motive, although it made sense upon her matter of fact confession. It went some way to reasoning why people tend to end up with partners perceived to be of their approximate equal value, however this value may be perceived. I also accepted a housemate, a fellow activist from my university days. As I was solely concerned for company, I did not expect much. This is what I got.

I augmented my social life by venturing out when opportunity arose. I got on board occasional kayaking excursions organised by my former university's outdoor adventure club, usually joining the group as they passed on the nearby highway. I joyfully reciprocated this generosity by offering budget camp stays to the club, sharing time trekking in the hills, canoeing and socialising.

These adventures also brought opportunity for relationship. Claire enjoyed the outdoors and equally enjoyed a challenge. She was and probably still is an intelligent individual, top of the class and beyond. She shared a sincere application to chosen disciplines. She expressed rare honesty, seemingly unconcerned with what others may think. She displayed a dispassionate disposition. Perhaps in this way we were too similar.

There was clear mutual attraction upon first meeting. Pursuant to this, I undertook what in retrospect constituted a strange path of behaviour. I went off and pondered how I was to seduce her, when she was probably already sufficiently interested to accommodate a direct approach. I avoided physicality until I had hatched a plan of an outstanding activity which could facilitate the move. Meanwhile she was wondering what was going on. I know this because she inquired of a friend, who in turn relayed the information to me.

I schemed a trip away together. She played along, though immediately after our bodily consummation, she retorted, "Are you happy now?" The ordeal I made of this exposed the folly in attempting to impress others. To do so is unimpressive. This behaviour carried echoes of a childhood conditioning that instilled ideas of personal insufficiency, of being an empty vessel to be filled. Again, as with Krista, the experience succeeded anyway. Nature's generosity continued to display its determination. The relationship, however, did not last very long.

∞

During the early years of my tenure, a new state government grant scheme introduced limited legalised gambling within its borders. Legislation imposed upon new casinos mandatory payments as a percentage of profit in support of operations established to benefit the community. As the camp was recognised as one such operation, I was able to successfully bid for asset acquisitions that in turn increased the camp's activity offerings year after year. Canoes, abseiling gear, ropes courses and a flying fox were added to pre-existing archery and orienteering equipment.

This culminated an ability to provide week long and multi-day packages to upper primary schools. In turn this increased the interest and occupancy of government schools which increased our income to the level of covering costs. It made it possible to hire competent outdoor instructors, friends from university in fact, to live on site and help out in running activities. This was the significant boost I needed to cross a major threshold. It brought my original dream into physical view.

The lifestyle was fruiting. The years began to move on through cycles. During the first school term and the first half of the second term we became fully booked. During this period of the year schools were not prepared for in house activities such as sports day, concerts, fetes, awards ceremonies, and thus relied upon the offerings of external institutions like camps to provide value. As schools sought consistent formality to ease their work load, all such clients booked similarly year after year, all well in advance. This provided us equally reliable income projections. We made most of the profits required to cover annual costs during these three to four months.

At the end of this period the year moved into winter. This was a blissful time of cooking on outdoor fires and sleeping out under clear skies filled with stars in the company of my closest of friends, now my work colleagues. We brewed beer, prepared elaborate meals, and established a garden. We invited visitors, trekked, enjoyed the natural surrounds and ventured further afield, all the while attending to more occasional guests and on-going maintenance, research and development.

Our created home-spun culture was founded on a pre-existing trust. It provided a joyful work environment from which our guests benefited. It allowed the opportunity to achieve much professionally and still provided vast amounts of free time to imagine and plan for more.

I pondered a way to further improve my lifestyle. I decided to monetise activities I was already enjoying in my free time. So began my DJing and party business. The camp was an ideal venue for such events with its 100 bunk beds, two large halls, and plenty of outdoor space for installations, bonfires and such like. These parties started out small, predominantly populated through the presence of friends and acquaintances. The events quickly increased in size and thus provided more to manage. The experience as a whole was to invite significant personal questions and incubate juicy paradoxes.

re-membering

∞

Early on the first night of the weekend of a party of unprecedented personal and enlisted communal innovation and organisation, all appeared as ready as could be reasonably expected. This event was quickly accumulating the largest turn out yet. Guest numbers were approaching 500.

It had only become possible to operate at this scale due to the co-operation of a Brisbane-based party-organising DJ syndicate. They had heard about previous parties at the camp through the spread of word-of-mouth and were impressed with the place as a venue. These guys advertised and promoted throughout the capital. They arrived days early and attended to much detailed preparation in a labour of love. Lights and decorations were up and running. Accommodation had been organised. All had been fed. The stage was set.

I was able to arrange time on the turntables prior to the visiting DJs taking over for the rest of the night. I was instantly joined by an appreciative dance floor. A group of musicians, inspired by the setting, ambience and response, soon approached and inquired regarding the possibility of performing. In my desire to maximise the potential for entertainment and participation, I arranged for a replacement on the decks so I could negotiate with the band.

The next DJ played his signature techno which changed the atmosphere, cleared the floor, leaving the band discouraged and of changed mind. This chain of events had the net result of lessening the variety of entertainment and participation, as in the process I had abandoned my contribution. Further, through the forfeiting of that opportunity to channel my unique musical inspirations, the party had lost an initial inviting segue into those more intense sounds originally planned for later in the evening. In the aftermath of that quick burst of situational irony, I was left standing denuded of an easy distinction between service to self and service to other.

I was not to return to the decks that night. There was too much else to attend. What I hadn't foreseen was the extent of my responsibilities. I began to feel much as out of my control. I was indeed relying upon the good will of strangers and the absence of factors that may collude to bring about undesirable outcomes. Many of these young guests were from the city, unfamiliar with nature's asymmetries and potential dangers. Most participants indulged in various forms of mind enhancing substances. Their care was my concern.

Prior requests for pills prompted the setting up of arrangements with unreliable suppliers. These middlemen commonly maintained an undisciplined personal relationship with the products they provided and this, in turn, kept them out of pocket, in no position to cover their investment. Despite conventional wisdom, in the interests of the show's success, I paid the price.

During my party wanderings I often spent time in transit on the dance floor. Considering the size of the crowd and the amount of mind enhancement, there were surprisingly few others present in the vicinity. More broadly, there were very few engaging in any form of overt self-expression. Were they enjoying themselves? Was the experience doing them any good? Was it doing them harm? There was a visible lack of communal celebration. There was little evidence of felt freedom. I recall coming across a considerable number of university acquaintances gathered around a fire on the other side of my residence. They had built a huge conflagration fed with timber that I had previously set aside for future construction projects. They stood in silence staring vacantly into the flames. One intoxicated guest went on an exuberant adventure around the lake shoreline, paying a visit to guests at a neighbouring camp. The manager punched the guy.

∞

These home events spawned gigs and engagements elsewhere. This meant much less responsibility and considerable compensation. These gigs begot more of the same, resulting in a stimulating flow of varying venues, indoor and outdoor, near and far, city and country. Outdoor events tended to offer a greater range of ways to enjoy the occasion, greater space, nature to explore, multiple music venues, fire places, performances, and no time constraints. They also provided distance from the objections of neighbours.

This flourishing party culture combined the ancient and the modern. This was the post-modern. Music technologies were advancing so rapidly that it was challenging to remain apace. As CDs replaced vinyl, vinyl releases became rarer and more expensive. Though CDs presented a different artifact, a lesser aesthetic, an inferior experience for the old school DJ. Digital audio files were just around the corner, presenting an utterly immense diversification in music sources, as well as innovating, mixing and playback options. On the ground, the culture borrowed much from exotica past and present. Tee-pees were common place, chai tea a regular refreshment, vegan and vegetarian food popularised, fire shows and drumming regular features.

∞

re-membering

It was an especial exhibition of adept fire-twirling in a suburban backyard that drew me into my next experience of the feminine. Her hips moved as to skirt the fires that flared on each end of the pole gyrating to the rhythmic pulse of the music. The resultant aesthetic was a staccato shimmy, moving up and through her voluptuous curves and generous bosom, culminating in a flick of her long hair. If the movement had not been consciously choreographed, then it had surely been unconsciously passed down through generations, eras and epochs from female to female. This was Eros. Or perhaps the Siren.

I was impressed. I was aroused. I wasn't the only one to have noticed. There was no time to lose. The painful hesitancies that characterised my experience with Claire were fresh in my memory, overwhelming any resistance. I let lust lead.

Upon completing her performance, she turned around and met my fixated gaze with matching lingering intensity before dropping to her knees and engaging her company in conversation. Feeling satisfied we had sufficiently communicated mutual desire, I moved inside the nearby dwelling and its lounge, feeling this to be a more convenient setting for rendezvous. She soon entered and walked to the centre of the room before turning to face me. There was a group of girls across the counter that separated a kitchen, though I cared not. I moved in, pressing my lips upon hers and in a continuation of the momentum, pushed towards the privacy of the entrance hallway. Our abandoned reciprocity made way to a change of venue. We quickly moved back to her house, into her cluttered bedroom, pushing all items off the mattress until no obstacle remained. Thus began a tumultuous, mysterious relationship, replete with intrigue.

re-membering

An inner-city dance party was the site of our first organised night out together. I noticed she did not reserve her alluring displays for someone uniquely special. It was not long before she was sharing a prolonged eyeballing with a male across my line of sight. I interpreted the exchange as delivering a single message, the same message that preceded our late-night activities on our first meeting. I walked out of the derelict building that constituted such a fine venue for this event.

I leaned against a brick wall and pondered my imagined situation. We had not as yet discussed the nature of our relationship. I did not wish to stop seeing her. I had not before participated in such enthusiastic sexual posturings. I was not a guy that suffered jealousy greatly. I considered my options, feeling things are rarely black and white. This liaison presented the potential of much abandoned physical pleasure and novelty. In broadening my perspective, I may allow further valuable experience, I reasoned. After all, I lived out in the country and she expressed enthusiasm in visiting. She lived in a beautiful old inner-city house and was happy for me to stay over. She occupied her abode with three other girls whose company I enjoyed. The arrangement provided further colour. It diversified and increased my appreciation for the spectrum of possibilities.

I came to a decision. I would not mind what she did in my absence. Problem solved, I looked up from my internal consultations. She passed into my field of vision and then halted, facing away, though the angle of her stance still accommodated a view of me through her peripheral vision.

We saw each other weekends on rotation. We did discuss our relationship in time. She denied any involvement with other guys. She wished to identify as monogamous. So now the issue was trust. We continued. She called it monogamy. I privately accepted she may not be honouring this term, but in the absence of evidence to the contrary, I remained willing. My mixed feelings fed a tension adding further fuel to our already inflamed sex life.

What was with her? Was she aware of what she was doing? Perhaps there were two unacquainted sides to her. Perhaps there wasn't. Perhaps she knew what she was doing, and cared not. Perhaps something happened during her upbringing. What if she was born that way? Perhaps it was her nature. Maybe she was divine, delivering calibrated challenge towards an accommodating candidate for the purpose of his beneficial development.

It became increasingly difficult to embrace her without accompanying suspicion. I occasionally caught glimpse of urban acquaintances shooting her a disapproving glance. On occasion she supplied what felt as overly wordy defences of personally insinuating circumstances to which I was neither privy nor prying. I extended my distance. I was perhaps contributing to our demise by design. Though I did not so much mind of that potential outcome. We had exhausted our cycles of negotiation. Any more of that would have simply integrated periodic dispute into the downward spiral that the relationship had become.

It was at one of the smaller parties I often held for university friends and friends of friends. It was during a set of DJing when I noticed her exchange prolonged glances with a guy before turning her head indicatively towards the direction of the house. The pair vanished. After allowing a little time and distance, I sought out a housemate to take over on the decks so I could be free to investigate. With my heart pounding and in haste I raced over to my dwelling. The couple had been held up at the entrance by another acquaintance who often lurked there during such events. I moved on without catching any incriminating activity.

re-membering

Again there was no clear evidence, however the persuasive circumstances triggered the rising of emotions from my dark depths. Towards the male in question I developed unprecedented anger. I understood my issue was primarily with my girlfriend, though this did not change how I felt.

∞

One afternoon while visiting friends at their home in the city, this guy was present. I glared at him with what I could only describe as a murderous look. He looked petrified for a moment. He then cowered, as if as a mouse.

In that moment a battle had been won. In that moment I was informed I too could be a terrifying individual, and naturally so. It dwelled within me.

This realisation made sense. Of course we have this potential. We would not have survived through the ages without it. For this occasion and for the entire experience, I feel greatly appreciative. It left me in awareness of my own danger, more aware of the entirety that dwells within me, more confident I had everything I needed to achieve all I wanted. Without this experience I would not have known of such an essential personal feature in a life worth fighting for. It magnified and personalised the force witnessed in the rural community through their own unreserved behaviours.

I felt like I needed to integrate this destructive force and make use of its considerable energy. Its presence immediately revealed old habitualised perspectives and behaviours now inappropriate in the meeting of every challenge. I needed to let go of old ways no longer of service. This did not appear a small task. It appeared to be of the magnitude of a cathartic incineration and subsequent reinvention.

∞

My dabbling within dance party culture was as much inspired as an invitation to embrace and share in a collective letting go. In this context it did not appear to be achieving broad success. Individuals appeared to hold firm to imaginary constraints. For much of the time I danced alone or in small groups. Patrons often huddled as they doused in substances not appearing to enhance their positive experience. It was as if many were labouring under the illusion of some potential negative consequence, or perhaps under the weight of responsibility the realisation of freedom presented.

What I offered didn't appear enough to some. Certain individuals wanted to avail themselves of resources not on offer. A situation set up for the purposes of providing for all was providing equally for those who wished to provide solely for themselves.

Of course, I did not know of the backgrounds of the many players populating this period of experience. The little I did know suggested no justification for negative judgment. Perhaps overt celebration was too much of a leap, or felt as unnecessary display. Perhaps, on the contrary, some were too much drowning, busy merely coping, and if so perhaps to avail of a life raft upon which to take a break would temporarily suffice.

My inspiration was being eroded by degrees. Was I looking for a non-existent tribe? Was I receiving feedback from these people suggesting they are not who they seem to me to be? However, I was not so concerned in them as presented. I was more interested in their potential. I was not going to give up.

Though it did appear there was much more to being of meaningful use than I had previously imagined. The experience was showing up my own misunderstandings and shortfalls. I felt a strong encouragement into a more fearless, fearsome, centred foundation from which I could speak and act my mind amidst all circumstances.

Meanwhile, my sexual relationship was approaching its finale. Its true nature appeared not to be about to reveal itself. Or perhaps it already had. I heard rumours not all was right with her housemates. She decided to move out from her shared house. She moved into a downstairs room at another location complete with private access through a backdoor and side pathway.

It was at this juncture I decided on a clean break. I did not only end the relationship. I relinquished my work agreements with my friends, closed the businesses, quit the job, walked away from my country home of 7 years, left my social circle, packed the van and headed south. I planned to sing about my experiences.

music and mayhem

I arrived in Nimbin in the manner of many over recent decades, in a vehicle containing all of practical material value, and without knowing where I would live. Also as many before, I had the convenience of a van within which I could comfortably sleep.

My first adventures here, now already 20 years passed, were still fresh in my memory. On the ground nothing much appeared different. The main street maintained all of its previous wooden facades, though now weathered in proportion to the time elapsed. The village remained quiet. It was late afternoon.

I parked on the road that led down to the bowling greens and caravan park and onwards towards the mountain range to the east and beyond. Glancing through the passenger-side window, I noticed an additional café had opened under the old building that formed one side of the village's small central square. This presented a comfortable place to relax prior to beginning my search for suitable accommodation.

re-membering

I scanned the room prior to entry. There was a stage at the far end. The large space between the stage and where I stood contained a brought-together collection of found, second hand and handmade objects that provided seating, both upright and reclining, along with items to be admired for their aesthetic value. The place was empty of customers.

Upon turning my head to the right, my eyes fell upon a woman. I hadn't felt her presence prior to that moment. It was as if she had disappeared into her activity. She was moulding plasticine between her long fingers. Her tall frame was trained intently on her creation. Her hair full of curls, her activity, her playfulness, reminded me of a young girl. It was her posture, her focus, her air, that felt of a woman.

I entered and moved to a table immediately to my forefront. She approached, and in doing so revealed her more formal occupation. I requested some coffee. She went off to prepare it. I sat refreshed, roused by the beauty of this female.

I then checked myself. I had come to Nimbin for the sole purpose of making music. This singular focus acknowledged time spent elsewhere is as much resourcefulness lost to the activity. The intention sought to remain conscious of the short time available in a life; the aim, to make the most of the opportunity availed. Reinforcing of this resignation was an accompanying recognition that I had just left a relationship which had led to significant compromise. Unresolved questions called for exclusive reflection and understanding.

My coffee soon arrived through the auspices of embodied service. She was glowing, as was I. I was left pondering this meeting's irony. And left it at that.

∞

re-membering

Robi has a presence that demands attention. He appears the sort of character that sees through pretence. I found him on the kitchen floor, slumped, his back against the cupboards that made use of the area below the kitchen sink. He hadn't bothered to move since the time I had shouted my original "Hello?" from the veranda that made up half the ground floor of his beautiful wooden house. He had responded after some delay, "Yeah?" with a reserved tone carrying itself as a warning. It was a clearly measured response, suggesting if I want the experience to go well, I need to respect I am in his territory, and should present myself honestly and efficiently.

Standing at the threshold of the open double doors, I requested entrance in a tone intended to convey the necessary respect. Robi's frame was mostly obscured by the cupboards that wrapped around the front of the kitchen and thus separated it from the foyer. The announcement of consent further prompted a keen sense of alertness. My welcome remained provisional, probational.

After reaching a position in the foyer that allowed for a full view of his large frame, at a distance that represented a compromise between non-intrusion and self-respect, in the midst of my personal introduction, I slowly dropped to my haunches, bringing our eyes close to level. I sensed something was not right with him. He felt as a wounded beast. He avoided eye contact, although my feeling was that he did so in order to remain focused on the gathering of intelligence, avoiding unnecessary distraction.

In the early exchanges little time was spent on the business of renting his house. Once my fundamental interest was established, the subject of the verbal exchange moved to my motives for my arrival in the region. All the while his intelligence gathering apparatus appeared to hone in on gauging my integrity, alert to any incongruences in my overall presentation.

It was only after a prolonged period, at a time beyond the setting of the sun below the tops of the surrounding forest, only then had it become clear I had been accepted as a potential tenant. The subject of Robi's conversation had slowly shifted from the initial probing interrogation, through cautionary accounts of past tenants, on to descriptions of the dwelling's design and its maintenance requirements.

During the proceeding tour of the house, he began to explain details of the construction, from the timber cladding to the solar power system. In the process he revealed not only his considerable knowledge, but also his passion for the subject matter. I appreciated his attention to detail, his respect for materials and methods, his desire to know. It encouraged careful listening, timely well-worded questioning, and responses in kind.

Beyond the tour, Robi's communications became more personal. Stories began to flow relating his impressions of the local community. His response to his prior social experiences seemed to have distanced him from the herd. He outlined many of the ways he had learned through which people can create problems. He saw human behaviour as commonly motivated from a deeper level of thinly-veneered ulterior motivation. He spoke of the masquerade of niceness that often shielded an otherwise needy, graspy intent, intent guarded by a malevolence that reared at the threat of exposure.

Robi painted a rather bleak picture. I couldn't disagree, though I had had not only negative experiences. Through my travels, my cloistered years, my time at university, and through all that had transpired since, all those interactions and exposures had etched a diversity of social perspectives, enough of which, I felt, to maintain at least some faith in the potential for some level of constructive communal co-operation.

re-membering

∞

I got started immediately after moving in. I sat surrounded by my newly purchased equipment, including digital recording unit, studio speakers, guitar, microphones, headphones, an effects programming unit, and all the leads that connected them. I purchased all with a portion of the funds that had flowed in and accumulated in return for my prior managing, catering, instructing and DJing.

I had arranged the purchase through a single friend, Andrew, a musician, a music shop employee of knowledge and influence. I trusted him. This made the process a joy, one that could have otherwise expended much time and energy. Our relationship had built steadily through the numerous social engagements that took place at the camp. Andrew came and performed with his band on a few occasions. He obviously enjoyed the chance to get out of the urban landscape, to enjoy the relative freedom and the wide-open space. I valued and nurtured this type of relationship, mutually beneficial, in service to inspiration, feeding further future potential, ultimately immeasurable in its synergistic benefit.

I picked up my guitar. I struck a single string. Instantly, a rich layering of tones emanated through the speakers. A single sound containing the many. My mind is cast back to my first experience in sonic exploration. Now, as then, I proceeded to survey the soundscape through the placing and intensifying of focus. The emanation was at once a fully realised completion and a palate of rich possibility, reverberating, alive. It revealed that in order to produce works of art, the process was at once as much one of forgoing distractions, as it was of choosing from within resonating options.

re-membering

The phenomenon of audible waves is obviously nothing new, not to the universe, nor to nature, and thus not to humanity. Objects resonate at multiple frequencies simultaneously, producing tones and overtones, and thus harmony. As white light contains all the colours of the spectrum, similarly on display here, the overtone series. Tones and their relationships are consistent among objects, and in relation to each other. As each sound has a tone and overtones, chords may be found emergent within a single note. Thus, music has its origins within nature. It is not something we have created from nothing.

As the sound faded, I struck the same string once again. Again I honed into the layers of sound, this time with an ear to create, shifting locus from created to creator. Starting with the fundamental, the lowest frequency tone within the sound, I began investigating overtone harmonies and exploring various combinations. Specific configurations suggested moods, moods drew feelings, feelings became my guide. Harmony presented accommodatingly, in accordance with where I resonated. Melody emerged as feelings proceeded to express themselves through time.

I pressed the record button. Individual overtones continued to offer themselves as sonic equivalents to outflowing emotive presentations; specific overtones pre-nominated as future fundamentals; and once sourced and highlighted continued to align, adding to what was now becoming an emerging story, a melodic rendering of a tale there to be told.

I conveniently relocated selected sounds among the 6 strings. Notes on opposite strings often combined in ways that provided greater body, more power, more persuasion. Within no time I had a progression. I grabbed pen and paper and, somewhat laboriously, noted notes, drew diagrams of the fret board, drew hand configurations, and improvised chord names.

re-membering

My aim was for a product that satisfied an imagined quality of wonderful. Wonderful, rather than excellent, as what I sought was the bewonderment of the listener, not something to be measured by comparative levels of high achievement. Wonderful is eminently possible, it surrounds and flows through us, it is available to be channelled, and re-broadcast. Feeling plays on the imagination, moulding figuratively, with all devotionally re-presented within a soundscape. Faithful re-creation beckons necessary skill development by its very nature. This mastery takes time as the physique must first be subjected to discipline if it is to become the loyal instrument of the spirit of music.

My present occupation had been inspired since childhood. Perhaps by the not so uncommon, yet mysterious, attraction of the musician's life. Music is compelling. All cultures include it as an essential part of their expression. Even monks chant. Yet immersion in this art is not logical. It makes no sense. Music has no desired destination. It is enjoyed as an end in itself. This suggests not all of importance in a life can be explained.

This does not mean we are willing to give up what is deemed logical. We do require shelter and food. But once housed and fed, what then do we do? It is as if we were born to express ourselves, to be creative. Creativity by its very nature arises in us through unfiltered inspiration. Thus by nature such expression is mysterious. Musicians are its subversive embodiments. In contrast, that which forms rational expression is considered trialled and thus true. It has history. It has served others in the past and pre-tends to serve similarly in the present. Unfiltered creativity, on the other hand, tends to service of higher-level aims, transcending of the mundane interpretation of a life.

I saw my opportunity within contemporary music culture and industry through its potential for novelty. Within the well-accepted principles of melody, harmony and rhythm the possibilities appeared practically without limit. This perspective had been assisted by an emerging post-modern resourcefulness, fusing elements of past musical traditions, combining these by and with the latest of technological capability. Music could easily be offered in non-conventional time signatures, songs could fade in at one point and end at another without the need for recognisable verse and chorus sections, sounds of individual instruments could be seemingly seamlessly merged in ways difficult to differentiate by the untrained ear, acoustic instruments could be juxtaposed with and against electronically programmed accompaniment. It was with an eye to combining these possibilities that I went about composition.

∞

It is widely known music forms a central role within alternative community culture, non-commercial, innovational music that finds its influences in many of the world's traditions. In this live and raw setting, diverse players follow along through cyclical, repetitive jams, allowing individuals to add further colour through soloing. In the absence of assertive mentoring and considerable experience among assembled players, the music can, and often does, become dense with the relentless non-practiced sounds of participants trying too hard. Add to the mix the often-non-harmonious combination of alcohol and marijuana, and what bursts forth often climaxes in cacophony.

This was my often experience of the local community's monthly music night. The atmosphere and its individual components gave cause to fascinate on the social chemistry that made these gatherings so special. All in attendance were refugees who had fled the city, most nursing their own unique scarring from an unkind past. Although the exodus is commendable in its motivation, its intention, its will to adventure, it also prompts a curiosity regarding how much each individual continues to harbour resentment of past tyranny, haunting their present attempts to get along with others in their new found community.

At one end of the spectrum may stand individuals who, through disciplined heart and mind, strike out with a single-mindedness, housing a clear vision of an evolved self within preferred surrounds, with a willingness to train in love's compassion, or at least tolerance and acceptance. At the other extreme remain those unco-operative, rebellious or dysfunctional, stubbornly holding out beyond their arrival in the promised land. The milieu of my experience came together in ways suggestive significantly of the latter. There was an insistence upon freedom, yet not always an ability to make productive use of it, nor to respect the freedom of others. Sometimes an inability for any insistence was on display, some appeared to float around offering mere mumblings, socially-uncalibrated utterances.

This was a petri dish of the unformalised. A welfare net allowed for the financially-secure roamings of many that would otherwise simply have nothing saleable to offer the market place. This alternative community had little of leadership. Seen as authoritarian, potential leaders were often viewed suspiciously. At times mere suggestions could be met with angry opposition. It's not that nothing was ever organised, but generally events asked little of their participants. Houses were cobbled together, gardens were co-operated, though often when government payments arrived, activities postponed in a haze of smoke.

Was a will to community harmony being confounded by the lack of mastery among its component individuals? I could not believe this is how people wanted to be. Perhaps there dwelled a perfection in the higher-level perspectives of this community. Perhaps this was a coming-together that prioritised the re-development of personal sovereignty over and above the development of the collective. Does not life equally exist and develop within the stagnant ponds that sit on the edge of fast-moving streams? I sought nurture through nature's metaphor.

When I was first invited to a music night I was thrilled. After being exposed to the disharmony, I sought to be selective in choosing with whom to play. Ultimately it led me to aspire for more. I was not willing to handicap my own progress. I wished the company of musicians of integrity. I sought musicians that displayed evidence of a desire to prioritise improvement over the buttressing of old wounds. I sought a collective willingness to sacrifice for the opportunity to play according to the accepted rules of participation. I enrolled in the nearby conservatorium of music.

∞

Obvious in retrospect, if music is the priority, hang out with those who are willing to give up their resources for the opportunity. The conservatorium had a first-year enrolment of around 35. This number pooled sufficient players in all roles of standard band composition. Two drummers and a number of bass players providing important foundation, guitarists and keyboardists providing body and colour, a horn blower and a wealth of vocal talent providing melody and story.

Although the conservatorium building showed its age, its heart was beating with youthful vigour. Cracks were showing in the building's red brick structure, though inside its many rooms, through its pianos, drum kits, amplifiers, mixers and microphones, music sustained its life. All that was required was to ask, and without exception, co-operative arrangements were effortlessly made. Musical theory and past experience allowed for unencumbered communication. A respect for the priority of music production transcended the politics of personality. Expressed performance anxieties were overwhelmed by the prevailing gestalt. The spirits of music were alive and well within the walls of this grassroots institution.

Wednesday mornings bracketed the week's highlights. This was concert practice time. Mandatory for all students was to provide a minimum number of performances during the semester to which feedback would be given. With two years and levels of enrolment present, total numbers exceeded 50, providing much practice, inspiration, enjoyment and entertainment.

There was so much music that playing became the social currency. Aligning with and within this spirit was gold, it was heaven. This zone became an increasingly regular location, although never certain. There remained countless ways of falling out, and much fewer, perhaps only one way, through which to truly remain.

At the end of term, a performance night marked the assessable culmination of the preceding months' progression for vocal majors. Mid-year required two pieces to be performed usually with the support of fellow students through their instrument of specialisation. Accordingly, negotiations were finalised and practice reached peak. At 37, with greater life experience in comparison to the other vocalists, and a desire to assuage any nerves on their part, I volunteered to begin the evening's festivities.

I chose self-written compositions in order to further my occupation as a singer-songwriter. The first song was intended to be the simplest in structure and so mildest in challenge in order to provide ease of entry for both myself and my accompaniment. The second song called upon players of more substantial experience as to render a performance of a greater dynamic and sophistication.

All went swimmingly. Notably, a personal commitment to promote an atmosphere of calm and joy for the singers yet to perform facilitated an absence of personal concern. There were moments during the second piece where I gained vantage beyond my physicality, as if to view my performance from above my normal line of sight. My fingers felt as if to move with an intelligence of their own source. The ungrounded confidence that flowed from this pinnacle of my life's musicianship was to set the stage for what was to come.

At the end of the year these performances for vocal majors were to take place again, although this time three songs were required. Inspired by what had passed at the end of term 1, I planned on raising the bar. I chose songs requiring more sophisticated guitar playing, a greater vocal range and diversity of emotional delivery, and further accompaniment including some electronically programmed additions. My preparations began with earnest.

My recording unit provided the ability to prepare demonstrations of songs I had selected to perform, both with all desired instrumentation and without specific accompaniments, the latter allowing space for selected players to practise along. I then secured the players, promptly availing them of my pre-recorded demos on computer discs. The musicians who had contributed to the successful performance at the end of term 1 were conspicuously unavailable due to popular demand for their services elsewhere. For this reason, I had to pick from a smaller selection of less accomplished players.

During the rapid passing of time leading towards the event, my visitations upon these chosen musicians revealed certain individuals had not yet bothered listening to the demos I had provided them, let alone come up with any ideas. Of course, excuses were offered. I felt the need to increase my encouragement, to sit through a greater than anticipated number of rehearsal sessions. Yet preparations still remained unsatisfactory. I saw the problem as a lack of discipline rather than any issue specifically musical in nature.

On the night the auditorium was packed. Obviously, my imagination was not the only one inspired through the success of the first term performances. The size of the crowd amplified an already long incubating sense of personal insecurity which until that point had remained in hiding, obscured by an arrogance that felt this as a triumphant moment ready to be seized.

I was to perform later in the program after a short break. When the time came, I was informed without notice that the break had been cancelled. This meant that the setup and sound checking of all instruments took place under a bright spotlight and a mass silent gaze.

I may as well have been naked; such was the extent of judgment I was projecting in to the eyes of each and every individual present within the darkness. A single encouraging voice arrived from the shadow. The doubt I felt was evidently visible. I felt trapped within my body, caught in a struggle to maintain validity, relevance, authenticity. In the absence of a pre-determined tribute, without dedication to an object of faultless external significance, by default, I found myself inadvertently split in two, partially a fragile fallible figure on a precarious precipice, partially a predominant overlord subjecting that reflected stage-bound image to a relentless merciless self-scrutiny. The surveilling tyranny sucked its vitality directly from the performance. I had effectively abandoned the muse, now condemned to try, and err.

Again the first number was to be a quieter piece, plucked guitar and emotive voice accompanied by a fusion of violin and violin synthesizer. My fellow musicians supported well, though while I remained intensely self-conscious, my voice remained weak and distant, as a fragment desperate to impress the all else. The second piece, intended to be a rousing celebration of a life re-discovered, ironically lacked power, now for the understandable same reason. The last song, performed with large band ensemble, was an absolute disaster. Drums entered belatedly; lead guitar slovenly. Flooding emotions found external targets upon which to project blame. Though the show must go on! I continued, my face reddening with righteous rage. The crowd felt the need to display increasing sympathetic support. Though the performance was dashed. I had been ambushed once again. This time a stubborn expectation had refused to recognise issues of rightful concern while allowing irrelevancies exaggerated import. The stage had been set for the spectre of chaos to find its traction, meaning and impact.

∞

Beyond the community of dedicated musicians the conservatorium afforded, I had also been gifted knowledge of what and how it is to sing in a technically correct manner. Prior to this training I had no clear measure of the part of vocal production not open to negotiation, and thus neither was I aware of the part free for unique aesthetic interpretation. Much of the course otherwise concerned with music theory and language: scales and the chords harmonised from them, chords and the way in which they are combined in order to produce progressions, verses, choruses, songs; and how such compositions may be notated in written form, providing sufficient information including tempo and rhythm, so others may accompany or replicate.

There had also been information provided on the business of music. This presented a picture within which I could imagine myself, to try on for size. This picture was framed from the point of view of the industry, its bottom line and how that intimately relates to the marketing of saleable product. There was talk of how musicians should package and arrange themselves in order to appeal to a certain section of the market.

I pondered the gruelling long-distance touring, dressing rooms and endless demands for repeat performances of the same material. I considered the pressure of recording deals with their requirements for the regular release of similar material based upon narrowing perceptions of what sells. Was this the requisite lot of commercial success?

An income would be required if I was going to remain free to concentrate solely on music, though sustainable commercial success is clearly a rare luxury. I had heard on reasonable authority that only the top 10 bands in the land earned enough to support themselves independent of other streams of income, and this often only on the back of a level of international success. Within this industry, musicians required an insatiable hunger, a willingness to place success above all else.

The business of music again presented paradox within my endeavour, a not shallow tension between authentic personal expression and the distraction of popular appeal and its monetisation. The extent of this dichotomy potentially presents nothing short of mutual exclusivity, as different as the activity of left and right brain. It would be highly unusual for a single individual to remain adept in both the artistry and business of music to the levels required to achieve sustainable success in such a competitive industry. This is one of the main reasons artists have managers.

As far as I was concerned, all considerations of self-promotion were anathema. I was not willing to market myself in accordance with a fashion, neither compromise my behaviour in a way that aimed to please an audience, or limit myself musically to a narrow style. In short, I did not possess sufficient desire for success on such terms. To attempt to do so felt fake; the reward, adoration and idolisation for something I am not. That's weird. That's empty. That's alienating. That's not so uncommon.

Of course, success may be measured in different ways. Personally, if anything, it remained a measure of alignment between creative inspiration and product, something that is relatively assured, in contrast to popular recognition, something never certain, of spurious motivation, and ultimately, as I had only recently been reminded, a seduction of potentially ruinous consequences. It appears the only healthy means to maximise the potential for a fulfilling, economically-independent musical career is to necessarily welcome favour and organise remuneration without being corrupted by it, at all.

∞

My year at the conservatorium passed rapidly. I had much enjoyed playing in ensembles. Music revealed itself as essentially a social activity, a medium through which players harmonise, so audiences may too harmonise, move as one, each rejoicing their own part in their own style.

The way forward was now feeling much more like collaboration. I ultimately desired a consistent community of musicians within which to thrive. Though I realised I would need to earn the right to such continued company through my own creative output. If I produced material of sufficient appeal, this would solve all issues regarding musician accompaniment, I thought. In this sense perhaps musicians were no different to individuals within the business and the community at large. Everyone yearned to ride that band wagon.

As my formal education ended, writing and recording continued. What I had learned of musicianship in the past year fed back into a general improvement in the quality and efficiency of my productions. My new short-term aim was to re-produce demos of my most market-friendly songs in order to seek play and wider exposure. My original imagined niche remained, that of providing interesting innovation within the existing alternative music scene coupled with lyrics contributing differing perspectives on the human experience.

Meanwhile the global scene was progressing as the new millennium turned one. During the period since I started producing, other bands had become renowned through the very same innovations that had been motivating my sense of uniqueness. Every single one of those ideas were now on display globally, embedded within the compositions of others. It was as if ideas come to many simultaneously, as if ideas are not especially personal nor original.

I recall my enthusiasm taking a hit. I was reminded of my absence of hunger for success as statistically measured. I was not one for which music was everything. I had nothing to prove. Further, I did not enjoy the air that surrounded ambition, of those who were seduced by the prospect of fame. Music was essentially something I picked up for the fun of it. I could just as easily put it down. Even though I saw the potential within the medium for sharing perspective, there were other means.

What remained was a child-like joy of playing with others. I availed myself of all reasonable opportunity. This period provided some of the best musical experiences of my life. At festivals, markets, bars and private gatherings; indoors, in tents, in forests and wide-open spaces; day and night; to crowded venues, to small crowds, with fellow musicians, to nobody; guitars, keyboards, drums and voice.

re-membering

∞

One morning while sitting within my studio, I felt an impulse to do something I had done little since puberty, and not at all for well over a decade. I turned on a radio.

What I heard was a news report of a significant global event. Without hesitation I climbed into the van and drove to the village in order to seek confirmation. All televisions in the hotel were unanimously tuned to repeating footage of civilian planes directed into collision with the upper reaches of high-rise buildings.

The only precedent within living memory this event could evoke was that from cinema, of the apocalyptic, action, drama thriller. And as the art of movie-making draws heavily from the archetypes, this too resonated with such depth, symbolically reminiscent, stirring within the unconscious, eerily instinctually felt within the otherwise shelter of my forest hideaway.

That original impulse had carried no moral flavour, ominous though nothing necessarily suggestive of malevolence, clearly as of something re-soundingly consequential. The weight of the event turned out as unprecedented in its scale, organisation and co-ordination, dark in its mystery. Yet this is being broadcast through a news programme. This is surely no dream? This is no movie.

This felt as an event so significant as to recast the context of a life. It surely changed forever how the nature of this world may be felt to be. It appeared to bellow vulnerability and fragility to the masses from a place beyond conventional notions of power and influence. Its effect was to surely smash through habitualised internalised monologues. If there was ever to be an event to cause an awakening, this was it. This was an opportunity for those able to be woken to wake.

This event cast doubt upon the very mechanisms of civilisation. I had never before given exhaustive consideration to who or what such complex human structures ultimately serve. During my roamings I had found the post-industrial cultures to be co-ercive by nature and thus not directly encouraging of individual human potential, rather rewarding acquiescence through negatively-geared incentives, withholding embarrassment, mockery, shaming, exclusion, isolation, alienation, in return for behaviour in service to external authority.

Such cultures tend to condition individuals towards a complex of rote reactions that over time co-alesce into a persona mistaken as a somebody, and through the admixture of euphemistic rhetoric, manage to perpetuate an experience mistaken as a self.

The system works so well that citizens co-operate to slavishly keep each other in line in the hope such actions may signal virtue, provoke positive appraisal, temporarily increase kudos and bolster the illusion of security.

In the absence of an explicable vehicle to wholesome self-development, individuals are left to merely speculate within the culturally conditioned limits of an externally projected consensus. There are no other socially acceptable modes of behaviour. To not act accordingly is to risk accusations of losing the plot. I guess that is literally correct. Yet there are many plots.

Within the plot of so-called capitalist democracies, or 'citizen-ruled investment for profit' schemes, it is of primary importance the majority populous remain hopeful of increasing monetary returns from their labour and financial activities. To this end, individuals need to believe they are being represented in government decision-making. This drama plays out through the infantile adversarial posturings of a ruling class of uniform career politicians who vie for popularity at the expense of personal vision. At the same time, such politicians attempt to garner campaign contributions in order to maintain advantage within this societal class, spending much of their time publicly justifying concessions to their industry funders they were appointed to regulate.

And so the voting majority casts their ballot towards the party offering relatively preferable financial conditions, commonly vowing less taxes. But regardless of how much holdings are increased, their value is governed by the percentage they represent as a proportion of the total pot. And so the more the rich inevitably distinguish themselves, the less value the poor must relatively hold.

What remains unclear is at what level within or without a civilisation's hierarchy do operations move above and beyond into spheres not driven by threats and falsehoods, where positive benefits flow as unadulterated co-operative service to self. Perhaps the true circumstances may elude analysis. Any attempt to accurately answer this question requires access to all relevant information. In its absence the most significant of benefactors may remain in the shadows. The vanishing point for the curious commoner appears somewhere in the vicinity of the media moguls managing societal narrative, the financial institutions manipulating monetary systems and the industry in production of weapons of intimidation and other such key tools and commodities.

re-membering

Whichever the true nature of contemporary human systems, I clearly felt the cultural edifice within which I negotiate my existence was undergoing a seismic shift. Long standing concerns resurfaced regarding humanity's obsession with the material and its insatiable hunger that relentlessly converts our life support system into items destined for discard. The scalpel-like incision of Science's blinkered reductionism and Christianity's insistence upon heaven being somewhere other than here combined with the cumulative sociological effect of neglecting respect of the world's inherent value, integrated existence and unitary essence.

The prevalence of these ideologies represented an unsustainable civilisation in necessary decline. Summarily, this prompted a revisiting of personal questions concerning a lifestyle appropriate to the times.

∞

I had heard of a newly establishing community nearby. The stated aim of this community was to offer a lifestyle independent of mainstream society, and thus to cease support for humanity's destructive trajectory. The consensus narrative amongst all present respected a love of earth and a concern for its care. The nominal guiding ethos was to follow the heart, in other words, to do only as you truly feel. All of this sounded sufficiently sound. I stowed my gear and moved in to take a closer look.

The site lay next to a clear, rocky stream that flowed around its eastern and southern boundaries. To the west, the land rose from an alluvial plain to a road that connected and serviced the surrounding area's small villages. The land's carpet of grass spoke of a recent history of cattle grazing. Large amounts of scattered refuse inclusive of rusting vehicle hulks spoke of subsequent occupations by several short-term inhabitants. The present community sheltered within a circle of tee-pees pitched upon the flat area next to the stream, mother, son and family, with the addition of a small group of predominantly formerly urban young adult males.

As a newcomer, I remained relatively quiet over the early days, more interested in getting a feel for the individuals with whom I now aspired to develop familial relations. Similar to my approach to activity at the temple, I went about doing the most obvious things I felt would contribute in a positive way, no matter how small. I attended to daily necessities, assisting in food preparation and clean up. During the day I chipped away at cleaning up the site. Also similar to life at the temple, there was not much constructive activity flowing from the other members of the community. Here however, there was much talk and much smoking of ganga.

Within the considerable free time available, I took opportunity to develop myself in ways neglected through years of living within society's convenience. This convenience had led to so much dependency. It had neglected the training of an ability to survive without it. Now this had become a concern.

I desired to understand how to live from and within nature. Though I had little information available to guide me. Reportedly, the continent's early white explorers found it difficult to survive without the help of the black fellas to guide them. In fact, some famously didn't survive. In the present era, black fella lore appeared also to be disappearing, with most of the locals purchasing items at the shops just like the white folk.

An ability to survive in the bush not only rests upon sourcing sufficient nutrition, it as much hinges upon the avoidance of toxins. These are very common within the native flora. Seeds, leaves and tubers may all contain unhealthy concentrations of such compounds. I knew I had to be cautious.

As a guide, I was armed with a single generic publication on Australian bush food, and thus I did not possess much information specific to the region. The book did however explain a suggested method of approach through experimentation. This method of touching, tasting and ingesting in increased amounts allows the body time to react in an informative way. Essentially each activity is carried out with a time delay in order to discern any adverse bodily reaction before proceeding.

On my food-finding expeditions I invariably wandered off on foot in the direction providing of the most undisturbed territory. Beyond the eastern border of the property, beyond the stream, the bush expands onwards through bordering conservation areas and national parks. This is mountainous terrain, the southern section of the Wollumbin caldera, the outer rim of a 23-million-year-old extinct volcano. The caldera circles its remnant plug of resistant solidified lava at a radius of some 20 km. Its elevation forms a shield to the coastal plain.

The area centring on the plug remains of importance to the Bundjalung nation, containing sacred sites including places where initiation rites were once performed. According to the culture, women are prohibited from climbing the peak. Rather spookily, I can attest to almost losing a girlfriend off the top decades prior. After slipping and sliding down the slope towards the ledge, it was but a single tree sapling that stood equidistant of her approaching parted legs that stopped her progress.

There are a number of well-established tracks that lead through the broader forested landscape, making for potentially days of uninterrupted walking. I increasingly left these tracks in order to accustom myself to navigating the natural terrain and so to accustom to less visited areas. My training increasingly involved the identification of familiar distant landmarks as a means of orienting myself when off track. The position of the sun also became increasingly useful as a compass during the early and later periods of the day.

An enduring landmark of the greater area remained a valley that ran west to east, opening to the horizon beyond the coast. I often lay down to pass the night on outcrops overlooking this valley. Here was an open view of the night sky, of the stars and the occasional moon when clear. Although alone, I felt without concern, nurtured through the agency and as a part of the immeasurable force that is Mother Nature.

Summarily, food sources were not abundantly obvious. There were very few signs of small animals, and even if there were, their trapping would require further research on technologies useful to that end. Flowers and fruits were also scarce, though, when located, often passed the test of edibility, thus enabling my role in the spreading of seed. Underground tubers were available, though required much preparation, soaking and cooking. Tuber chemistry facilitates a plant's secure storage of food, the starches remain inedible, the nutrients locked up, inaccessible to predators, until such time the plant enables use of the stored energy through a simple conversion to sugar. Over time it became increasingly obvious insects were perhaps the most suitable of staples due to their abundance, ease of collection and relative suitability as a safe source of nutrition.

As a group we, the community's men and boys, initiated shorter night treks. We chose against using flashlights and went barefoot. My barefoot training had been developing ever since I had returned to the continent, through my university years, most thoroughly through my years at the camp.

re-membering

The sense of touch this afforded informed path choices. When the ground became uncertain, toes became active in investigating the ground before resting the foot and shifting weight. Going barefoot restated a balance between navigation and intelligence gathering, and created little disturbance. This latter outcome was not a moral choice, it happened naturally. The cultural standard that had become the wearing of heavy-duty boots in such terrain resulted in relatively no feeling, not only removing so much information regarding what passes underfoot, but also of destruction caused. An early discouragement to going barefoot is the prevailing softness developed and maintained though long years of wearing shoes. Softened feet are obviously vulnerable to pain and this underlines what is lost through the choice of convenience of any kind. Convenience breeds increasing intolerance. Once barefoot is resumed, feet soon re-harden.

Eyes became less the priority sense on these nocturnal outings, although there remained a peripheral vision, seeing to the detection of subtle changes in shades of darkness, serving as a warning of impending obstacles such as branches within the arc of vision. The olfactory sense came alive through a palate of ambient aromas, from leaves and floral notes, through intermittent scents of humus in decay, to more subtle not easily identifiable suspensions. Ears trained towards the direction of coming and going stimuli, carried within the ebb and flow of air currents, the sound of flowing water, the rustle of leaves and the rubbing of branches, at times providing orientation to more open ways of proceeding. The skin provided an informative interface through keen sensitivity to temperature and pressure variation, from the often warm, heavier, moister air that cloaked the thicker vegetation of the low-lying gullies, to the thin, cooler, draftier, lighter areas at greater elevation.

As a general experience, whether alone or in a small group of focused individuals, these types of outings are fulfilling. As much as they present as an exercise in skill development and group co-operation, the activity remains a joy in itself. The feeling is of an immediate dissolution within the living world. Nature beckons. An emergent harmony induces the sensitivity useful to navigate through otherwise unpredictable terrain. The senses merge and intensify as an experience in all things as one thing. Within this melting of boundaries, concern is diminished for the physical, and thus too diminished, the concern of mortality.

∞

As with many who joined the wave of new arrivals to the Nimbin region since the 1970s, individuals within the community were also sourcing fortnightly payments from the government. After payment day the young males would routinely disappear, off to enjoy the inebriation money so easily affords.

One evening I was sitting enjoying the quiet within one of the tee-pees. I was alone due to the rest of the members being either away or out in the village. Just before midnight I heard the approach of a small group of humans. There were the familiar voices of two of the young males, and a third unfamiliar voice. They were obviously drunk judging by their louder than normal, drawn out, wavering vocal cadence. They bashed through the canvas door and stood around exchanging comments regarding their night's sojourn. The third figure was a young black fella, perhaps in his mid-twenties. He was acting quite arrogant and aggressive. He insisted I tell them a story. Through evoking the prevailing community ethos, I declined, not feeling to give into duress. The guy reacted with anger, escalating quickly to a torrent of wrath. He began to rant, leading to a crescendo deep and dark. Accusatory descriptions arrived of his aunt's beheading at the hands of white men during the earlier colonial period. His tone carried on vengeful and murderous, evoking a sense my life may be threatened. Machetes lay around, and I was unsure of the valour, commitment nor competence of the other youths to de-escalate the situation. They remained silent.

In a state of induced transcendent awareness, I slowly raised my body from its former cross-legged posture before walking it to the door and out in to the pitch darkness. I was unsure of where to proceed. During the period of time it took for my eyes to accustom to the new moon night, I pondered my options.

This was my rightful home. I did not feel to run and hide. So with a sense of abandonment to fate, I simply entered another tee-pee. There I lay down. I closed my eyes. A loud buzzing energetic state of heightened frequency within my ears accompanied a resigned focus. I proceeded to quickly vanish, completely. This was beyond the by now accustomed absence of identifiable personality. This was a total absence of identification with the body. I became pure omnipresence, invisible yet still intensely there. And, by the by, this consciousness passed into unconsciousness.

∞

As much as I recognised external subsidy as a factor in the undermining of the community's priority, it was not the most significant portion of my concerns. It wasn't something prohibitively impeding of the potential for constructive development. Even the land existing in no part within my legal propriety I could accept. I didn't feel I needed to own something to be able to contribute to it in a healthily meaningful way. I hadn't owned land in the past yet I had been able to maintain and develop holdings of others, assisting the furthering of ventures I felt of value. I accepted the premise to exemplify a mode of behaviour contributory of a wholesome foundation for others to recognise and engage as sufficient.

My foremost concern, the deal breaker with regards to my continuing commitment to the project, lay with the character of the main land-holding family members, their many words, though few in relation to a detailed vision. The recurrent theme of the son's regular rants remained a passionate opposition to what he insisted upon as an existing conspiracy for world dominance among the ruling government and business elite. This, among the most common of his verbal offerings, he couched clearly as a matter of us versus them, expressed in a consistently vindictive tone. I had battled through my childhood with a similar anti-establishment attitude. Though I saw no utility in remaining adversarial beyond those years of externally enforced confinement. I was no longer being made to do anything against my will.

The antagonistic mentality smelled as a flawed pre-occupation for a sound community, especially in the context of an otherwise general lack of development towards a viable alternative, independent way of life. The attitude felt as lazy, lacking in creative inspiration. It probably conceals a level of envy for those it condemns, all the while remaining dependent on those same individuals for its very existence. The motivation appears to fulfil the need for a diversion, providing a scapegoat for personal feelings of ineffectiveness. Without excuse, the self-image may otherwise struggle with the uncomfortable revelation of its own responsibility for its own immediate circumstances.

The son postured as a man of unquestionable esoteric and worldly insight. He presented as beyond reproach, as a man who does not entertain dissenting opinion easily, as if this was especially virtuous. It made for a man difficult with which to reason. And driven by his stated belief in the ever-present threat of unscrupulous incursion, he remained of an imposing demeanour.

As the days passed I continued in my personal site clean-up initiative. With a mounting sense of time slipping by, I became increasingly concerned and emboldened in response to an elsewhere general stagnation. I took the opportunity to share more and more of the understandings I carried forward from my experiences abroad and since my return. I wished to motivate the young guys towards a greater contribution of creative ideas and constructive activity.

My sharing appeared to threaten the son's sense of unique authority. It was not long before he began to insinuate a very real threat of enemies within the group, as if to suggest there was the presence of the 'them' among us. This was soon followed by incidents of his physical trespassing on the small area I had set aside for myself in one of the tee-pees, his unapologetic boot-shod tramping among my few exposed possessions and upon the bedding within which I laid down to sleep. I had seen enough.

∞

With the benefit of hindsight, this community of my brief experience constituted very little of integrity. As such, I don't consider the place as an accurate representation of intentional alternatives in general. However, the experience ponders what may likely constitute the essential pre-conditions for the establishment of a healthy community. By their nature such groupings are complex, perhaps the most complex of all human endeavours.

Of course, humans do not hold a monopoly on such organisings. Curiously, the ecological school of science defines community to include all living things interacting within a location, not just those of one species, let alone a sub-set of a species. This definition nests neatly within the theory of natural selection in recognition of forms of life as not emerging in isolation, but as part of a whole, evolving so slowly, over periods of time so vast as to be difficult if not impossible to conceive, and thus of a complexity beyond understanding or replication. This suggests natural communities are born of neither intention nor design, rather as a small though inextricable part of a whole undergoing countless iterations of eternally morphing circumstances.

The human body may be considered a community. Specialised individual cells operate for their own continued existence and in so doing support the continued existence of the entire organism. The cell's survival is inextricable to the organism's survival, thus it may be misleading to distinguish them in a haste to make sense. By extension, the idea of a human organism acting like a cell within a greater population of humans may also question the validity of differentiation, at least in the context of the individual's survival being dependent on the survival of the population. The suggestion here is that the co-operation of groups is perhaps also achieved out of an on-flowing mutual biological necessity.

Human communities co-habit through the essential maintenance of shared abstract stories. Through these narratives, humans maintain the descriptions necessary for the patchwork attribution of an internalised identity. Identity may be conferred to the individual, the couple, the family, the team, the congregation, the race, the gender, the nation, the species, and so on, all conditioned towards the delineating of an entity for which an activity or a life is undertaken.

Within human populations there are specific sub-group identifications that perhaps thrive exceptionally, that is, in the seeming absence of immediate life-threatening motivations. Within the arena of team sports for example, members sacrifice towards a benefit of greater perceived significance, the team's success is held as paramount. Through individual sacrifice, personal identity expands as to be inextricable from that of the larger group. This allows performance to exceed that of the sum of the individuals. However, team sports may be contextualised as a practice in the art of war, and thus at heart, of concern for survival fitness.

Within religious communities, whether magical, mystical, or mythical in foundation, beliefs or faith inspire individuals to congregate under an authority of origins less effable though equally transcendent. Through the act of sacrifice to communal religious allegiance, individuals may not only appease concerns of personal fragility within an otherwise threatening world, but they may also placate concerns regarding a supposed afterlife. Immortality is the ultimate survival.

In the context of the human intentional community, survival is debatably a factor in the formation, even if motivated by but a perceived potential threat of broader society's terminal trajectory. Though this may not constitute a sufficiently imminent factor as to consistently motivate harmonious development within the offspring group. Such gatherings form, even by the admission of their members, as a choice, an alternative. Here, in the shadow of the coddling mainstream mother, in the absence of do or die circumstances, humans appear capable of a greater degree of inconsistent, at times destructive behaviour, of occasional unmitigated petty infighting, of wanton grasps at power, or of default apathy, simply because they can do so without placing their survival in jeopardy.

∞

And with this passed my involvement and interest in intentional community, at least for now. My experience engendered and fostered an appreciation for the complexity inherent within elsewhere functional human social systems. A respect was newly found for the prevailing worldly examples of scaled human organisation. History had overseen manifold attempts at such abiding synthesis, enshrined constitutions of extensive lineage, learned of precedent, accounting of countless findings from endless tribulations. Civilisation had come to somewhat buffer against the dangers of absolute power, had accordingly developed frameworks to guard against tendencies towards blind self-interest and malevolence in the extreme. Leaders had understood the need for transcendent principles and binding consequential agreements and plans in order to achieve productive outcomes and avoid argument, theft, bloodshed, or simply a waste of time and resources. They had developed independent arms of governance to make, interpret and enforce laws for the purpose of approximating the highest imaginable communal and individual ideals.

And with this respect came more of an even greater acceptance of and resignation to things as they are. As concerning as a contemplated prospect, my bodily fate remained awash within an ocean of blinkered, self-serving, material-hoarding, polluting humanity. Through alternative community, my vain attempt to detour from humanity's blindsiding of its own folly was met with more blindsiding and folly.

And with this resignation eroded the last vestiges of reason to extend my re-visit to the island of my birth. Most of my adult life here was spent on country, even my university experience was set within a forest. I will always love this land deeply. It is and feels ancient. It evokes the eternal. It invokes a dreaming.

The indirect benefit bestowed of this land's relatively small population of pre-dominantly recent arrivals pre-dominantly huddled near the coastline is an outback sparsely populated and relatively undisturbed.

The more time spent away from the abstract ramblings of a nation's urban cultural institutions, the less life is hijacked by story. The more time spent in the absence of such conversed notions, the more self is realised as nature. Within story I am a mere character, beyond story I am life itself.

And this, as direct and non-ideated, dwells beyond explanation. Explanation merely reduces to those same blinding abstracts that which is actually clearly ineffable.

a much-maligned re-creation and her immeasurable benefits

Social dynamics play out unconsciously more than is comfortably acknowledged. Behaviours are often conditioned rather than informed, habituated through long repetition, driven by prompts and directed foremost towards safety. Thus a rather elusive determinant forms significant part of that which constitutes convention.

Within my enduring desire to make sense of self and other, the us and them, I have felt cause to fascinate upon that which characterises essential difference between the dynamics of social convention of East and West. In my considerable experience of both spheres, differences appear remarkably polar, and so may be meaningfully viewed in contrast, even perhaps as two sides of a coin. By way of example, a foundation of personal relating in the West is consistently portrayed as a function of rights, in the East as that of service.

On the surface a rights-based system purports to bestow advantage to the individual, although such systems may evolve to limit the individual in order that actions of that same person do not impinge upon the rights of others. This leads to a tension. I have observed much clamouring to prohibit the actions of others in the West. This is clearly reflected in the many laws that purport to restrict community disturbance, in battles over civil rights, and even in legislation regarding what individuals may or may not do to themselves, such as in laws prohibiting the use of psychedelics and in the curious illegality of taking one's own life.

My realisation while at the temple represented the high tide of my life's understanding till that moment. From there I could no longer sincerely attempt to invalidate any behaviour. All behaviours have integrity simply as they are able to take place, as all action arises as an inextricable expression of the whole, and thus all action speaks equally of the whole of which it is a part. The whole would not be whole without all such parts, even if the whole is not wholly understood. Nothing occurs in isolation, and so nothing can be fully appraised without wholesome reference. To not acknowledge this is to unavoidably withdraw into ignorance. To acknowledge it is to remain free to enjoy all experiences and respond, or not, according to unfettered free will.

What I had been witnessing within broader Western society was regular intolerance often delivered with accompanying vehement emotion. In the context of culture, this non-acceptance disables the recognition and respect of differing beliefs that give rise to alternative world views and values, and thus contrasting community behaviours. Ironically, inter-cultural tension born of clashing ideology tends to only strengthen respective world views by granting each a counter, something to push up against.

Intolerance is generally symptomatic of a self-imposed limitation that now seeks to limit the actions of others similarly. Such prohibitions, unless aligned with genuine inspiration, produce a corresponding internal dissonance, and this is not something for which the behaviour of others may rightfully be held accountable.

Society appears to be made up of sizeable factions of humans who forego personal inspiration in favour of group conformity, complete with its prohibitive regulations regarding behaviour. So even within cultures, intolerance may persist through a common attitude that may be summarised as: if I don't do it, then I certainly will not accept you doing it.

The systems of service immediately evident in the East more directly subjugate an individual's sovereignty for the sake of maintaining harmony within the group. Asian cultures prioritise this service to family, authority figures, business affiliates, friends, though not so much to strangers. This is at the root of a posturing that, above all else, aims to please, avoids confrontation, does nothing that tends to risk an embarrassment or a loss of face for anyone concerned. Individuals sharing meaningful contact are spared words and actions that may otherwise threaten positive reputation.

These cultures thus discourage expressions of honest opinion. This behaviour befuddles the average Westerner's attempts to conjure a consistent image of their oriental counterparts, often resulting in conclusions of inscrutability or suspicion of disingenuity.

At the level of community, this oriental orientation combines to play out with less of the dissonance characteristic of the West. Though as a consequence this mode of behaviour motivates an underworld, a black-market trading in all things individually desirable though otherwise non-contributive to the smoothness of a greater societal functionality.

As inaccurate as this comparison may be, it remained my clear impression during my third visit to Thailand.

∞

I did not opt to take flight immediately. I had as yet neither the determination nor the sufficient finances. I first moved to Djanbang gardens Permaculture Institute on the outskirts of Nimbin village. Here I could recuperate a relatively healthy sense of co-operative living while remaining in tranquil rural surrounds.

The institute serves to educate in sustainable living, offering design courses that seek to provide hands-on experience in the maximization of production of necessary resources from materials grown and processed onsite; combining old and new appropriate technologies; integrating passive energy systems; and recycling for minimal waste; all in ways observant, learned and respecting of natural systems.

The 5-acre site contained dams top and bottom, with an established tall forest along the northern boundary, extensive annual gardens, specialised food forests comprised preferentially of endemic species, diverse bamboo plantings, and further room to accommodate pigs, geese, ducks and chickens. Fee-paying students are housed in a collection of retired, converted train carriages.

The director welcomed me to assist through maintaining the grounds, and as time passed on, increasingly managing volunteers and guiding visitor tours of the property. My move here provided a stable home life, a beautiful natural environment and the opportunity to be a part of a community of all ages and a diversity of nationalities.

In addition, I soon managed to secure employment for 2 days a month at a nearby market, on the day before the event setting up the car park, and on the day, counting the take. I later also found employment within a local organic donut enterprise riding a wave of popularity on the local festival circuit. Beyond an income, both options provided outings at which music could be played, as well as be enjoyed vicariously, with the latter providing opportunities to get away and enjoy different areas of the country.

As owner of the donut business, Phil had already been working hard in getting his concern up and running over the previous 7 years, so he was happy for me to share greater responsibility for stall set up and the management of some shifts. The donuts proved to be a popular breakfast option for early risers, though before the first daily donut was sold, dough required preparation and time to rise. This led to 5.30 am starts after 1 am finishes. Within the ephemeral celebratory atmosphere and our often-key proximity to live music, these long shifts were eminently doable.

∞

My new home base placed me in the situation of considerable sexual opportunity. Various engagements achieved varying degrees of development, though none consummate. As sex had never been a lasting priority throughout my adult life to this point, I had not realised the extent of my shortfalls in terms of an easy progress towards physical intimacy. Until now I had got by largely through a generosity of circumstances, succeeding largely from within a spirit of dissociative abandonment, often instigated physically through a disarray of clumsy leaps and lunges.

These new circumstances were not only highlighting a lack of embodied competence, more importantly they were bringing to the surface an accumulation of inhibitions. Granted the consistent proximity of sexual possibility, the corresponding corner of my mindscape was being repeatedly exposed as a realm long left unattended, long providing safe harbour for adverse imagery and ideas diverse in foreign provenance. Fragments of religious perversion and echoes of feminist disapproval piled upon other more commonplace misleading depictions of the female as sexually indifferent, fragile and fickle, all confusing a perception of a courtship culture already characterised by an uncertainty regarding where lines are to be drawn and re-drawn.

In this new found environment, confronted with this clutter, and in light of my specific insight training, I found myself in the habit of detachment, effectively escaping. The potential for confusion was causing default into a well-practised non-dual consciousness. In short, in situations of perceived intimacy, I found myself repeatedly abandoning my body, and thus neglecting of my sexual aspirations.

I was mal-functioning. There was so much I was ignoring of reliable imaginative inspiration and emotional intelligence, so much I was not saying, so much I was not sharing, so much I was not permitting in terms of a relaxed physicality, consequentially only serving to disable response and limit exchange.

I had now entered my 40s and as yet left unattended a level of general skill within the sphere of female courtship and affinity. This neglect formed part of a consistent lack of priority service paid to my individual self since my mid-20s.

All as much highlighted an immense sphere of pre-occupation so essential to life, yet one little discussed, less trained, and personally, till that time, practically little understood. If anything, such a topic defaulted towards the taboo end of the spectrum. It is as if the amount of conversation time sex gets within the public arena remained inversely proportional to its significance to our sexually-reproducing species.

Depending on the individual and their mood, sex may conjure memorably as pleasurable, sensual, passionate and lustful; enthusiastic, lively, exuberant, thrilling or jubilant; even giddying, delirious, ecstatic or euphoric. Fond are its recollections in satisfaction, satiation or fulfilment; inspiring are its motivations toward kindness, sensitivity and affection; welcome are its promotions of curiosity and play. Though allusion may rouse to the extremes of submission and dominance, where the passive, yielding, intimidated or overwhelmed meets the spirited, confident, cocky and strong; or the disturbingly aggressive, threatening or cruel. A mere insinuation may challenge the innocent, shy, nervous, uneasy, apprehensive or insecure; provoke the needy, yearning, infatuated, obsessive or desperate; promote feelings of misery or regret; remind of the frustrating or confusing, painful or devastating, jading or empty. Echoes may haunt the possessive, jealous, envious, resentful, embittered, vengeful, cowardly or pathetic; invoke feelings of shame or guilt, loneliness or fear, anxiety, panic or anger. With all this potential, it is understandable the irrepressible drive has not received the widespread conscious consideration contributive of transparency and characteristic of a more enlightened society. Sex remains a hot topic and for good reason.

Within the context of human culture, historically societies have sought to regulate the sexual activity of their offspring in attempts to maximise the fitness of their descendants. Until recently, parents have sought to influence their children's choice of mates towards marital circumstances that perceptibly serve best the perpetuation of a prosperous lineage. Upbringing of the youth towards a broad sexual knowledge and competence runs counter to this inter-generational imperative. Previous generations, even if well-intended in desiring the best experience for their progeny, had been equally left in the dark, discouraged from experimentation and left non-conversant in the nuances of the art form.

Even in an era of relative financial independence, efforts towards sexual prowess often remain socially challenged, presenting as an easy target for collective envy or competitive self-interest, with the potential to set off strong emotions, produce tension, and possible confrontation, all threatening to the average individual's precious self-image and general stasis, not to mention their physical health. Therefore, any will to knowledge emerges, not within neutral territory, rather within a familial and societal setting of strong discouragement.

To perhaps provide the most persuasive of contexts, evolutionary biologists claim sex emerged as a reproductive strategy over a billion years prior to the emergence of self consciousness and its will to cognition, in other words, an eon before any attempted ability to understand or inform it. The self that seeks sexual artistry begins life in the same condition as its distant ancestors, as a clueless offspring of a primordial instinctual drive. This self then proceeds through those unavoidable decades of marination within a sea of imposed culturally-endorsed antagonisms. Personal efforts start out from a self-identity accumulatively comprised of the inherent biases born of such past and present circumstances. Stepping out into the adventure is thus a recipe for much early confusion, heartache and conflict.

So to acknowledge my socio-biological inheritances was to simultaneously accept an actively diverse sex life as of a considerable worthy challenge. I duly accepted. I decided sex was now to be my priority, sex and all that comes with it, sex and a lifestyle that maximises the possibility for and potential of its experience.

I wished to honour this desire no less than all other inspirations that had previously motivated and continue to motivate my lifestyle choices. Sex was no longer to be a sideline distraction, or a passing enchantment. It was to be as central to my life as it is central to life.

The aim was to develop a working conversance with the dance to the point of it not being an issue, to the point where attraction prompted behaviours that faithfully represented my interest and contributed to the most favourable circumstances for each encounter's flourishing. The prospects filled me with excitement.

The strategy was to begin again, to set a blank canvas. In order to simplify things to a level of optimum manageability, in order to provide most space to adopt and play with personal characterisations appropriate to the desired style of engagement, a different habitat, one less of confusion and prior entanglement, felt the best place to start. I began to research cultures most suitable.

∞

The ambient sounds of sentimental romantic pop were unlikely to be first choice for any of those gathered, not for the customers nor the proprietors. Though I doubt anyone cared. My company consisted of a couple of foreign males of an age beyond innocence, and our hosts, a couple who shared a thinly-disguised ruthlessness that lurked behind their exaggerated smiles. Personally, perched to the side of this combi van refitted as cocktail bar, located just beyond the old city's moat-traversing main gate, I felt without a care.

This was Chiang Mai, a destination chosen by Phil of organic donut fame. He was here for a dose of ozone, a blood-cleansing treatment illegal in our self-proclaimed free country of birth. I had already short-listed Thailand by the time Phil had mentioned his plan for a visit. Thailand, South America, Spain - all presented as countries appearing to highlight lifestyle over career. It became a simple matter of expressing an interest in accompanying him at the time he was arranging his itinerary.

After paying our bill we set off casually down the moat. It was early evening. We passed a multitude of street vendors serving up made-to-order dishes to groups of diners seated around makeshift tables at the rear of the wide sidewalk. All ingredients remained on full display, exhibiting their freshness and facilitating an ease of customer choice. Many of the diners were drinking beer purchased from one of the nearby convenience stores.

The time of night felt to coincide nicely with the possibility of novel experience. The warm tropical air carried the pungent aroma of the region's well-known traditional spices, wafting in juxtaposition with the increasingly audible infusions of nostalgic Western music. We followed the familiar sounds into the bar of its source. The location offered comfortable outdoor seating, pleasing views of still waters, a pool table, and the friendly welcome of its female staff.

I got chatting with one of the girls who spoke considerable Japanese. This amicable exchange seamlessly led to seating and continued banter. The convivial atmosphere impressed me as an early display of this service culture, a quality through which the business could surely only benefit. This was an institution where there appeared no clear demarcation between staff and customer. We were all celebrating together, the staff as hosts, and we as honoured guests. Nothing felt too much to ask. I felt as in a new home. The atmosphere was encouraging of play. I required little encouragement.

Just prior to midnight, Phil and I headed to a club. Again the moat oriented our passage. There were very few people inside the venue, but again the service was welcoming. I engaged in superficial conversation with a girl who promptly insisted I buy her a drink. In the midst of my polite refusal, I began to back away, only to collide with the knees of a further female seated in my path, ending up momentarily in her lap. My immediate apology she gracefully accepted, leading to introductions and an explanation of my recent arrival in the country. She offered to help me get oriented.

The club began to fill quickly after midnight. The atmosphere improved with this increase in numbers. There were balanced ratios of genders and ages. On the whole, people were enjoying themselves, dancing and conversing. All was well.

I pondered the contrast of my adverse experiences of Australian club culture as a teenager. The few venues I had attended back then presented as dark, noisy, unsociable affairs; the service impersonal; the atmosphere competitive and intimidating, tension often hung in the air; the need for security apparent. These negative impressions had formed part of a growing general dissatisfaction, and early reasons for my avoidance of popular culture.

re-membering

In contrast, this Thai establishment was filled with an air of fecundity, pregnant with possibility. Females in their numbers set the mood, unabashedly contributing to my visual, audible, olfactory and tactile impressions. Girls expressed themselves within their groups with un-self-conscious abandon, their voices delivered a nasally mid-frequency sound that easily and conveniently floated between the accentuated highs and lows of the music.

This conversational din spoke of a familiarity characteristic of a sisterhood, an intimacy founded upon a grounded practicality, a type of accord to which I had not previously been exposed. It was as if all they had ever known was communal living, as if there were no secrets worth holding. All the while the tone remained thematically reminiscent of adolescence, in its cheekiness, in its urging, in its seeming lack of concern for the morrow.

As this was not only my first outing within a new urban culture, but also within the culture's mating sub-culture, I was in no hurry to commit to new found company. As an observer alone, the experience was deeply stimulating. The form of the oriental female absorbed my attention for long periods - thematically petite and curvaceous, the smooth tanned skin, the long silky jet-black hair that fell about pert breasts, the rounded symmetry of facial features, those absorbing dark eyes.

My fascination did not stop at the obvious physical qualities. My examinations drew me to feel into the character that brings life to such exotic attributes. The exhibitions of easy, outward relating suggested an underlying open availability; a receptivity that felt to extend beyond the immediate social group subliminally messaged its opportunity.

My imagination began to entertain renderings of pleasing, slow-moving, sultry exchanges. The inadvertent sexual arousal this caused immediately drew responses; wherever I placed my gaze, heads began to turn; hair brushed aside; bodily contours highlighted. These responses consistently emanated a wellspring of invitation, passive though strongly seductive. After some repetition, a pattern emerged, uncomplicated; as if nothing stood in the way, as if this is how it was intended. I felt to be in the right place.

∞

The following day I woke to the sound of my hotel owner's voice. I had a visitor waiting for me in the foyer. Upon arriving downstairs I immediately recognised her, the girl I had met the night before who had offered to show me around.

Nina spoke little English. On my request, we went and purchased a Thai language text book and dictionary. If this was to be my new home, communication through the local language would be essential. As I had learnt from my time in Japan, culture and language are inseparable. To understand language is to largely understand culture. Language reveals the nuances of what is and what is not deemed important.

In Nina's presence I immediately found myself drawn in to the habitation of my masculinity, my physicality, my sexuality. It is hard to know how much each of us prompted such a chemistry; it just was. For her part, it felt as if she was open to anything. Her countenance displayed an easy readiness. Her language, both spoken and unspoken, consistently encouraged my initiative, its clear expression, and follow through. She looked upon me for her lead. It felt as if I was being called to step forth to fill a man-shaped vacuum.

I later found out one of the most commonly used expressions in the Thai language amply gives voice to this spirit of service. Literally translated, 'laeo dtae kun' (แล้วแต่คุณ) becomes 'already but you.' Fleshing-out the phrase arrives at a sentiment similar to: 'your wish has already been granted, except for your part.' This is certainly how it felt to be.

My part, my stepping forward, engendered visceral feelings of a filling out, like more of myself was being energised, was coming alive. I breathed into this vibrancy, slowed down; my centre dropped to my gut. This inspired more of a free flow within and without, an unleashing of spontaneity increasingly inclusive of all manner of creativity and expression. The result felt as a deepening sense of well-being. I quickly re-dis-covered a desire, a propensity, a natural urge to engage my singing voice; I had quickly re-engaged with the spirit of music. I cried tears of joy. She, in her straight-forward way of expression, said I was crazy.

Nina had a child. Her man had since left. She was now living back with her parents. I soon got to meet them. The family was very relaxed on my visit. After introductions they simply went on with their normal activities. Nina's father had throat cancer and had already had surgery. He showed me the large scar. There was more surgery to undergo, and little did I know, this was to be the reason that created the pressure that was to end what would develop into a short relationship.

It happened all of a sudden. She just stopped ringing and turning up, and eventually stopped answering my calls. At least I was belatedly granted an explanation. Nina was impressed upon to seek out the support of her ex-husband to support the family, and more immediately, help in the cost of her father's surgery. The circumstances delivered a brutally sobering glimpse into the day-to-day requirements of survival in this part of the world.

Without a welfare net, the family functions to support itself as a whole. It is thus understandable why this unit forms the most important priority to its members. The experience enhanced my appreciation for my own circumstances. Whatever I chose to do with my life, I did not carry the financial burden of my parent's survival.

Nina emanated beauty. In the presence of women like her, there is not much a man who recognises the opportunity she represents can not do. She is unconditionally accepting, and thus provides the space to encourage her man to do all that he desires, wants, is capable of, and beyond. More than giving of herself, she gives herself completely.

I wonder how much beauty emerges from within such situations, that is, from within the predicament of hardship. Obvious examples from among history's outstanding achievers float to mind - those community leaders, artists and sporting greats who appeared to have nothing or were willing to forego everything. There are many examples: Martin, Ludwig, Vincent, Billy, Diego, … Michael floats to mind; he shared beauty through his song and dance; beauty which ultimately engaged millions of adoring fans; beauty trained through long hours of rehearsal overseen by his father's whip. I wonder how many of those fans are aware of what he endured for the sake of their entertainment, their idolatry. Hardship and beauty remain a common association, though not always acknowledged, perhaps as mis-understood in their relationship as light and dark.

In contrast, I wonder if a life of privilege is in anyway preferable. This circumstance rather often robs people of the motivation prerequisite to the blooming of beauty. Rights personally unearned may excuse individuals from initiatives that would otherwise grant life such manifest meaning. Such rights tend to expand a sense of egoic self-importance at the expense of worldly achievement. Such rights may so easily persuade mediocrity. For such perceived entitlement, there thus remains the possibility of a high price. There may be no easier justification for dashing opportunity, for sitting by and watching life pass by.

If an equation may be drawn that links hardship, sacrifice and beauty, then a claim of rights in the service of excuse may equally equate comfort, apathy, and … well, ugliness.

∞

Phil and I soon began researching the potential of setting up donut operations in Chiang Mai. Competition was investigated, ingredients sourced, possible shop fronts located and costs calculated. Existing donut outlets offered low prices but typically overly-sweet, otherwise tasteless product. Ingredients were affordable but not of the quality we had been able to source in Australia. Available points of sale offered possibility, particularly in the area of street vending. Our retail price would not be cheap, though we considered this an acceptable compromise for the comparative quality. The question was more of affordability.

By now we had moved into a townhouse to keep our long term rent affordable. The three storeys allowed us plenty of space, and most importantly, a kitchen for donut production. In this tropical climate there was a need to experiment around the physics of rising dough. Obviously, the process would progress faster in these ambient temperatures. Donuts could still be shaped at the appropriate time, though the optimum window available prior to over-rising would be considerably less. There was also an issue with humidity and how this affected the character of the finished product. We continued trials and the results were good, though not great. A new savoury line was achieved through the combination of seaweed, tofu, wasabi and soy sauce as a centre.

We took a batch to the local bar of a friend of Phil. They were fine with us hawking among their customers. The response was encouraging, selling all product at each time of visitation. Although a lot more would need to be sold if the profit was to support even one of us independent of other streams of income.

The time for Phil to return home arrived. The consequences were something I could have foreseen if I had taken the time to think things through. Phil had signed off on a year lease on the townhouse, though he was no longer going to contribute to monthly rent after his departure. On the day of his departure, he left the place in a mess, leaving me to tidy up after him. There was his and his girlfriend's blood-stained sheets, dirty dishes and accumulated waste. I put on a show of anger, though in the end I was simply happy to see them leave. It wasn't so difficult to pick up the pieces.

I had a home, a small industry and an opportunity of a lifestyle. Over the following months I continued to make donuts and sell them at the bar. I was probably one of the few, if not the only Western hawker in the country. However, it soon became clear I would not be able to reasonably survive on the profits of donut sales alone.

I decided to seek employment in an area of high demand, school teaching. I enrolled to undergo certificate training. I did not know if this qualification is a necessary pre-requisite for finding suitable employment, though as an outsider to the education culture, I felt such a first step would help me re-acclimatise to the atmosphere of the classroom, preparing the ground upon which the responsibility of managing and facilitating the development of rooms of children may succeed. The course would not only place me in the company of those more familiar with the local system and its cultural peculiarities, it would also connect me with other foreigners willing to engage in teaching as a means of support.

The course ran for a number of months, brief considering the variety and level of skills required for effective teaching, though of a length desirable for individuals who were simply there to learn the minimum requirements for securing employment. Training could proceed on the job. In this context, not much was covered in terms of classroom skills, though generally the information helped in the most important ways. It informed of what is expected of a teacher, and of how to present accordingly. It informed of the types of employment available, and the resources needed to fulfil the role of educator. It informed of how to go about seeking employment, and assured of the likelihood of finding suitable placement. At that time, most foreign teachers in the country were without formal teaching qualification. I was told that for many schools it was important to have a foreigner on staff primarily to maintain appearances. This reportedly impressed the parents, simply because a native speaker of English was teaching their children.

For the first time since before leaving Australia at age 21, I sought employment due to a need for a stream of income. As I had only engaged in labours of love over the last 20 years, I quickly resolved to prioritise learning to love this occupation, to not focus on the money. This was essential if I was to flourish. I needed to find a way of making the experience into something I celebrated, something I genuinely embraced as an activity meaningful in its own right. I did not doubt it could be done. It did not feel that difficult a challenge in principle. Teaching and learning are such essential, indispensable aspects of a full life.

Specifically, I needed to treat the classroom and embrace the children as if my own. This would require the founding and maintaining of clear uncompromising boundaries from the outset. It would also require content be interesting. I could hardly insist upon co-operation if my lessons were not engaging. I needed to teach from my heart. I needed to teach as if the content mattered. This required to present lessons within the context of a personally ascribed meaning and value. Summarily, the plan was to do things my way, regardless of the dictates of the institution. I determined to maintain this strategy come what may.

re-membering

I found a job on my third application. This placed me in one of the largest private educational institutions in the city. The school was well resourced and the class sizes manageable. The children were mostly co-operative, though early on small groups of solely male students emerged as regularly disruptive. It took me around 6 months before frustration and occasional bouts of uncontrolled anger ceased to find expression in my performance. I remained solemnly determined to totally avoid recourse to the harsh punishment and not uncommon derision of my own upbringing.

I ended up with a system that warned individuals of the consequence of exclusion if they were to continue creating disturbance. Though if it came to sitting them outside, I made it clear the situation was not personal, it was done so I may teach effectively, and if they were willing to cease creating problems, they could return. The system worked well as no student wished to be separated from the group. Within this settled-upon dynamic, I developed lessons pitching a little above the average competency, encouraging of self-motivated students to extend themselves while embracing without judgment those who showed little to no sign of progress. And with this, classes began to approximate my sense of ideal functioning.

∞

Meanwhile, regular ongoing attention from females nursed a moving on from my previous relationship after a brief period of mournful dis-interest. The general receptivity of an opposite gender commonly endowed with such personally alluring physical features; regularly animated with such a lightness of being; relaxed, joyful and playful; with

[233]

a grace devoid of arrogance; and steeped in the value of service, remained consistently appealing.

Now single, I wished to keep it this way. I had not wished to be in a relationship to begin with. My previous engagement developed as a rolling on of consistently productive rendezvous, beyond the letting go of past inhibitions, into the heart of undiluted desire, expanding in to the rudiments of an uncensored expression. The liaison had delivered me back within my body, and it felt good. The combined and accumulative effects were powerful. I felt inspired.

Moving forward, I felt more potential rested with exploring variety, providing novel grounds for experimentation and expansion. There was indeed much to investigate, from the initial pull of attraction, through approach and presentation, leading to the appropriate means of engagement and communication, to levels of intimacy, and the inquiring of and expression of boundaries. The recognition of abundance within a sexual culture relatively free of complication remained broadly liberating. I had relatively little to lose. I had immeasurable to gain.

∞

I continued to celebrate the ease of lifestyle this novel culture offered. There remained a non-pedantic attitude to the rule of law. For example, if teenagers needed to get to school, they were simply allowed to ride there by scooter, always without license, sometimes without vehicular registration, often without helmets, at times three to a bike. This leniency further extended to those out for a drink in the evenings. There will be people who would find this situation unacceptable, but for individuals who favour a life of personal responsibility over state control, this feels more like freedom.

Though there also existed points of cultural difference that rather led to issues. For example, a social problem unexpectedly emerged within my street as the result of my visibly casual mating behaviour. Nothing was ever mentioned in conversation, though there was no other significantly dependable reason for such a radical change in neighbourly attitudes. Within the cul-de-sac of my thin dividing wall to thin dividing wall accommodation, relations had begun quite cordially, especially on the part of the married couples. Though behaviours soon morphed. Neighbours increasingly displayed a clear indifference to my presence. Over time this intensified into a commonly visible disdain, and then physical displays of passive aggression such as parking vehicles across and eventually within my driveway, escalating to active attempts at intimidation through the lurking presence of a number of the younger males of the community.

The situation represented a fundamental tension between the local culture and my ethics. The locals are no less likely to engage in casual sexual liaisons, though such dalliances are managed with discretion or even secrecy. No doubt this maintains the family environment free of the visible evidence of destabilising influence. My neighbour's avoidance of discussion on the issue echoed the importance of the avoidance of confrontation in general, the priority of social harmony, and the associated matter of saving face.

I viewed the situation with a respect tempered by an acknowledgement of limits to the significance of culture in anyone's life. My own drenched cultural experience of my childhood had already been contextualised and thus downplayed by later worldly experience. The maintenance of culture is essential to survival of any community, though survival is not an end. That game never ends. Personally, survival was never a good enough justification in and of itself. I had already realised I am more than a personality within a culture.

What I was doing would not damage these people, the community would endure. I indulged a little of an occidental perspective towards this system's double standards, though balanced with a recognition of the pragmatism of the local mores and an acknowledgement of my place as a guest within the country.

∞

Abundance does not necessarily confer any specific characteristic within a lifestyle or any specific trait within the person. Setting off into an ocean may equally lead to drowning or to washing up on the rocks as it may lead to learning how to swim and delving the depths.

With regards my relationship experiences during this period, I could say I had learnt to swim, though I also became increasingly aware of the small eddy within which I splashed; one within which I had plumbed little of the depths. I remained a novice in a wading pool full of a specific breed of fish. Sure, I had shed those previously culturally-conditioned impositions, enjoying pleasure and in the process finding posture and voice, though I had developed little in terms of a broader worldliness and aptitude.

My social circle now centred around a weekly pool competition; the venues invariably Anglo-centric. It was not only the game; the soundtrack was also of Western origin. These venues naturally attracted girls who shared an interest in foreign men. Beyond the novelty, a taste for the exotic, the cultural curiosity, the freedom from the strictures of the familiar, rightly or wrongly, Western men were commonly seen as good providers, even if only evidenced through their visible spending patterns.

It is perhaps interesting to note that the majority of these females were from the countryside. Many of them were the daughters of rice-growing families. For me this availed them of a certain immediate appeal. These girls, brought up with their feet in the dirt, called upon to assist rice planting within knee-deep muddy water; of often sinewy physique and of skin accustomed to the sun; of simple taste; and an unabashed, unaffected tone, made for hardy, happy-go-lucky company in most situations.

Many city girls made efforts to distinguish themselves from their rural sisters. Through obsessing over the whiteness of their skin, often to the point of lathering themselves in bleaching products, many were keen to signal they are not the offspring of poor farming families, but rather the offspring of ways and means. Though, to my eyes, often these girls looked pasty, unnatural; of a paleness suggestive of ill-health. Further, as a consequence of their self-conscious efforts to signal class, it appeared a significant portion of these women sought the company of men willing to afford them the outward displays of wealth they valued. This game smacked of the superficial, the dis-ingenuous; materialistic, and not much fun.

It was not uncommon to hear certain city girls express befuddlement at why so many foreigners favoured their rural sisters. What they probably did not understand was that most of these foreign men, being already of sufficient means, cared little for further material acquisitions beyond immediate practical utility, let alone for their public display as a means of signalling affluence. Further, as urban females did not tend to offer any greater opportunities for philosophical interaction, then for most foreigners, desire for female company was often satisfied through an uncomplicated, relaxed, affectionate type of relationship.

As most of the country girls possessed a working knowledge of functional English, there was no apparent need for conversing in the local dialect.

Equally due to the ease of communing, there was little need for the developing of sophisticated social skills. As comfortable as these circumstances were, I knew this was not where I desired to remain. Events tended towards repetition. Novelty tended towards its exhaustion. I desired to get out and explore beyond the limited social circles of expatriate Westerners.

In order to maintain a trajectory towards broader assimilation, I continued to study Thai. I regularly sat on the roadside on mid-week nights translating the menus on the fluorescent street vendor signs with the help of a dictionary. I began to only choose the company of girls who did not speak English. Of course, this furthered my fluency in the language, though more importantly it maintained an increasing feeling of being at home within the culture. I attempted to explore a wider variety of activities and conversations. Though come the weekend, I continued to frequent the same bars and similar resulting experiences. I knew I needed to modify my lifestyle, though I equally knew this would require breaking new territory. Something had to give.

∞

It was a particularly dark night. The sky hung thickly blanketed with low hanging clouds. Rain fell lightly, though of sufficient volume to keep me undercover. I resigned to head home anyway. I pulled on my helmet and mounted my bike. Soon after moving off I opened the helmet's visor as it had begun to fog from the warmth of my own breath. I kept my head at a mild tilt in order to avoid the spattering of raindrops into my eyes. My mind shared the mild foggy characteristic of the ambient atmosphere. I veered off the moat road and began my run towards home. This road was absent of street lighting. The darkness, the sprinkling rain and my dull occupied mind combined to guide the tilt of my head towards the road about 5 metres ahead.

Suddenly I noticed small red lights in my upper peripheral vision at about 10 metres. Above the line of lights was a space where light was absent, pitch dark, more so than the surrounds. I applied the foot brake lightly to avoid sliding and losing control. It quickly occurred to me I would not be able to stop in time. I added the front hand brake. I slid. Upon impact my right leg was thrown forward and hit the bumper bar of what was a stationery waste collection truck. The bike fell to its side. The labourers standing beside the truck looked on, though remained still.

With only my arms for support, I raised my torso and began to pull my body free of the bike. I continued to slide myself towards the side of the road. Meanwhile the occasional vehicle drove towards, passed and beyond my outstretched body. From my vulnerability I yelled to the crew now continuing their activity around the truck. No help was forthcoming. I redoubled my efforts, dragging my body backwards to get myself to the curb, up and on to the footpath, and finally rested my back against the pole of a chain-link fence.

I fumbled for my phone and scrolled for someone of a heart to assist and of the local knowledge to make that possible. I decided to ring a girl that I had been seeing for a while. She would probably be able to arrange an ambulance. I explained the location and then waited amid the continuing soft drizzle of rain.

A van arrived within half an hour. The staff managed to place my injured leg in a wooden splint, place my body on an army-grade stretcher, and then load me into the back of the vehicle. At the hospital I was x-rayed and then left to rest in a room of three beds, having been granted the berth next to the large exterior window with its commanding views of the city below.

re-membering

The x-rays revealed the obvious. I had sustained breaks to my fibula and tibia. Though there was to be a pain-filled overnight wait before an operation would be conducted. I was not prescribed pain killers. It was suggested such drugs may introduce unnecessary risk to life when it came to the complexing administration of anaesthesia prior to surgery.

$$\infty$$

I awoke after the operation euphoric. After a brief period of orientation, I guessed my feeling had been artificially induced. I had most probably been granted morphine. It re-minded me of sitting in that bungalow on that island with Aroon and Krista.

I was overwhelmed with a sense of well-being as if I had woken in to some heavenly realm. Staff came and went, beautiful girls in uniform flirtatiously tending to my comfort. Without hesitation their words enquired of my relationship status, the type of 'specifications' I prefer, before revealing with added gesticulations, viable candidates amongst the staff. All this exuded from them with an easy sensuality, humour, sensitivity and grace.

The girl I had originally rung to organise my rescue turned up most nights. She bought and brought bouquets of flowers, a smorgasbord of food and a variety of new clothes. She made routine use of her intuitive, sensory and inquisitive skills in the process of catering to my needs and wants. When her work circumstances allowed, she would share my hospital bed overnight. As the time drew towards my discharge, she organised temporary ground-level accommodation for me. This would facilitate my training in the use of crutches prior to a return to my 3-storey townhouse and its narrow and steep staircases.

re-membering

My hospital expenses were almost totally covered by insurance. The major source was a compulsory scheme connected with my employment, though there were two other streams related to vehicle registration. In order to qualify for some of this insurance I required a police report regarding the original accident. One of the employees of the waste management company claimed that I had injured him at the time of collision. I knew I had not come into contact with anyone during the ordeal, though I was encouraged to pay cash compensation to this guy in order to better the chances of a favourable report from the police.

After leaving the hospital and moving to my temporary accommodation, I spent considerable time accustoming myself to the use of crutches on the laneway outside the guesthouse. On one of these outings I met Lee, a girl from Laos. She was occupying herself teaching some of the locals English. Due to my lack of mobility, I was well pleased to have the opportunity to spend time in her company.

This girl was well educated, holding two degrees, and the daughter of a family with members working within the locally prestigious ranks of government. The family also owned a restaurant situated on the Mekong River in Vientiane. The perceived uniqueness of this independent girl overwhelmed my former decision to remain single.

When I eventually felt fit enough to return to my townhouse, after some hesitation, she moved in with me. After what felt at times as holing up for the duration of the full year contract, we moved to an apartment within a more inner-city location. This offered not only more privacy among a demographic less constituted of families, it also provided greater material security and convenience.

I remained keenly cognisant of the fateful significance of the motorcycle accident. As much as it re-presented a consequence of my lack of independent enterprise, it equally gifted a way out of a pattern of activity no longer serving, and led to this meeting and its potential. Beyond Lee's exquisite oriental beauty, I valued her liveliness, her determination, the freshness of the whole experience. So when the question of marriage arrived, I did not feel to quickly discount the suggestion.

Though in my subsequent reflections I recognised that in our time together we had not discussed in depth our important differences. We had not established clear channels of communication towards such a mutual understanding. At the times when personal opinions were aired, she remained consistently inflexible, favouring advice commonly sourced from magazines more than any personal experience. This had not constituted a barrier to the enjoyment of our informal domestic arrangement, though within even a mere hypothetical consideration of a proposed contractual union, this inability to find consensus or compromise appeared as fertile grounds for future irreconcilable conflict.

Functionally, from a solely re-generational perspective, marriage made obvious sense. Though from the perspective of furthering an individual's fulfilment, this traditional union appeared inconsiderate, as if the reproductive function was the fulfilment. After all, a priority of reproduction does not distinguish humans from monkeys, rabbits or even a virus. Yet humans like to regard themselves of superior intelligence. We have consciousness and self-awareness. Personally, these traits led to self-inquiry. However, this pre-occupation appears rare, and commonly at odds within the culture of marriage, within the culture in general.

re-membering

At the time, within the local context, a life occupied with the management of conjugal union and its spawnings appeared overwhelming: directing energy into the toil of resource accumulation and culturally-dictated familial activities; negotiating demands for ritualised displays of worldly success, photo after photo; social engagements populated of rehearsed conversation of no import, out of politeness, not of genuine curiosity nor desire to understand; behaviour directed by tradition and market forces; wave after wave of hard-shelled yet empty exhortation.

This most practised of social onslaughts felt as a disrespect of intelligence, as a disregard of the capacity to feel and think, and to speak and act freely. It appeared as a default to a form of automated operation: deferring to endless external insistence, and thus to a voluntary personal ignorance and its consequential numbing effect; foregoing the gift of creative response ability in exchange for the dictates of societal responsibility, mirroring of and for others in order that they may in turn mirror reciprocally.

Suffice to say, at that time, with that girl, under those conditions, it did not feel right to marry. I was not of a will to marry. I simply wanted to be with her in the way it already was. Though as the relationship's continuation now relied upon a marital commitment, it ended there and then.

∞

re-membering

After the breakup, I took a break, happy to focus on my professional development, relaxing socially in the company of light banter among my teaching colleagues, though with increasing ponderance on how to proceed.

Throughout the time spent within this companionship, it became increasingly apparent my fellow ex-patriates shared an in-common reserve amid females present and passing. Further, beyond this inconsistency in harmonious engagement, beyond the occasional opportunism, a myriad of behaviours of greater concern were on display, from an interfering competitiveness to rarer though more memorable eruptions into acts of wanton sabotage.

Amusing were the boasts of past personal achievement or conversely the belittling of others in a vain attempt at relative self-elevation; contentious were actions undermining of the greater group harmony; unsettling were the manoeuvres seeking to monopolise, cut in, or underhandedly engage; unacceptable were the malicious insults directed towards the anatomy of females present; provoking was the threat of indiscriminant physical violence indirectly bringing about an abrupt end to otherwise positive personal prospects, or the otherwise wilful destabilising of developments through the introduction of clearly intentional upsetting drama.

Regularly on show were behaviours of an undeveloped kind, the extremes of which more at home within the wilds of the untrammelled beast. The general situation suggested a commonality of cause, of upbringings and furthered histories of neglect in the ways of nurturing mutual prosperity. There endured a thematic lack of positively constructive conduct within an atmosphere of stagnating emotional maturation. These symptoms were reminiscent of an imagination prolonging of a cocktail of counter-productive limiting beliefs, ingredients combining to inhibit the heart and mind from the embracing of nature's fruits.

Whenever the topic of a specific incident was later broached, the reactions were almost entirely of denial, excuse or non-remembrance, all serving to subtract from the point of debriefing while adding to a revelation surprising in its extent. As to avoid the discomfort of vulnerability, it appeared preferable to eschew personal responsibility altogether, defaulting to the shelter of an armoured self-preservation, a behaviour no doubt honed through decades of immersion within the insecurity of similar company. Surely only harbour of questionable virtue is thus found, a defence through the protectorate that is mob affiliation.

Naturally, all the while, the energy of the powerful instinctual drive remains. Though able to be unconsciously redirected and degraded interiorly, and temporarily numbed through alcohol or such like, these energies are still ultimately triggered into expression on the next occasion of sexual possibility, whether manifest through a less dishonourable social insensitivity, or through a more aggressive action born of frustration.

The everyday experience of this incubating dis-position is no doubt the quiet hum of dis-satisfaction, if not despair. Unwilling to authentically express, the avoidance appeared to speak its retraction, the dishonesty its exploitation, the resentment its retribution. While this misery seeks company, energy is further routinely mis-directed in an endless striving to impress peers within a lonely herd hierarchy continuously treading waters of its own polluting.

My male companions and I had broken away, distanced ourselves from the environment of our earlier acculturation, though refusing, or at least struggling, to take the opportunity to pardon ourselves from the repercussions of that past routine subjugation. There was certainly ample evidence of a voluntary perpetuation of those prior unhappy impositions.

There existed little ease in the ways of genuine relating and co-operation. There was barely a ground of what may constitute a healthy, productive fellowship. I was embarking on an adventure challenged by my own lack of mastery, commonly finding myself at odds with my male company. I had envisioned a playground, though this one was of an adversarial character hauntingly reminiscent of my youth.

∞

A spectrum of feelings unfurled amid the witnessing of such incidents, general pity not least among them. The identification of this pity as a symptom of perceived victimhood called for an immediate non-compromising response. I viewed pity as yet another masquerade of cowardice, the weakness that feared confronting self-imposed hurdles to a personal fulfilment.

The solution was simple, that being to not indulge pity. This would require vigilance. Now a warrior stood in the midst of the imagination. One that was to stand guard against arising suggestions of the world being in any way to blame for perceived mis-givings. There is an external version of this warrior, one fearless against intrusion and conflict, one aspiring of impeccable standing, not desiring of physical confrontation, though disavowing excuse in dictating action.

It felt a little dangerous. It felt the ultimate liberation. In the absence of pity, there appeared only opportunity. It was as if pity had formerly been utilised as a justification for not taking on what otherwise presented as so much response ability, and thus a justification for continued inactivity.

Practically, I decided the whole project could be further assisted by removing or at least minimising unnecessary situational distractions and obstacles. Foremost, after my experiences within the broader social milieu, I figured the best way forward to be alone, once again, allowing exception in the rare company of co-operative individuals. In this way I could attend to my operation without feeling the need to compromise and complicate circumstances further.

Further, the situation called for a comprehensive review of my process, inside and out. This was to be a discipline, as with all sincere undertakings. It led to a thorough investigation of all within my ability to control. Beginning again from unified mind, that field of awareness complete with its inbuilt love of its own nature. Then to move within this space to the centre or feeling of sexual energy, to allow this energy to permeate being. Any intrusion on the part of apparitions that may otherwise transgress and cause to undermine inspiration, anything arising now no longer of use, the coming and going of emotions that seek to sway mood against desired developments, all are monitored and free to leave. This became the interior preparation.

Exteriorly, preparations set out from an honouring of attraction, its uncensored expression, attending to presentation, posture, body language, eye contact; providing offerings towards intimacy; intense yet relaxed, intelligent, calibrated, unintrusive. Freewill remains respected, atmosphere remains liberating, outcomes remain irrelevant, process remains the end. Summarily, all contributes to a practice in the free flow of sexual communication.

∞

This re-novation continues as a work in progress. The discipline that is this lifestyle is well-assisted by the avoidance of over-exposure to the broader community and its seemingly infinite variety of distractions, disturbances, objections, interferences, obstructions, and assaults. Time away from engagement in targeted experiences has been time well spent in solitude - when not consciously consolidating constructive behaviours through merging the imagination within activity; then resting, accumulating energy, exclusively prioritising the practise of the settled mind.

This is an enterprise of invitation, a joy grounded in awareness, love, desire, authentic communication, humour, and, a celebration of the female. Beyond the surprise and shyness, much new found company remains receptive. And beyond a mutual re-cognition of the nature of the encounter, beyond a tacit consent to its development, themes broached appear without limit - from the relational, through the ways and means of self-acquaintance, to the fulfilment of aspirations thus revealed. The child that first made strides through lived-experience is now called towards maturation via the unprecedented levels of creativity required to navigate such communications.

The realm of intimacy is rife with the most unexpected of circumstances, and it is these that have drawn the most out of the potential for all manner of novel development. It starts with the call to stand up. It continues through an insistence upon a shedding of reputational concern. It beckons a heightened aliveness and spontaneous innovation. It proceeds in curiosity through the courage of conviction. It motivates a navigation of the mysterious. It requires a responsibility broadened beyond the individual self. The child that first made strides through the lived-experience is now called into adulthood via the unprecedented levels of love and wisdom required in the exploration of this territory.

Within the context of offerings made towards physical union, so much is evoked as personal resource. The resulting innovations accumulate as much as a store of tools, and further, leads to a synthesising of spheres of activity previously assumed independent, bringing all movement within the world to a more complete functioning adaptability.

The sexual adventure is just as much feeding into an emerging fullness for all seasons, highlighting and attending to all aspects of the human vehicle, this conduit of experience, providing training towards a buoyant upstanding in the face of all manner of greater challenges. Few among the experienced would disagree, there is hardly an occupation so strongly motivating through desire, so committing to a value recognised through the power of attraction, so demanding through the unforeseen nature of its challenges, and so cleansing through its indiscriminant sweep of all areas of weakness.

re-membering

This story emerges from between the cracks of a joyless, unrelenting oppression. It begins at a time and place within which the long traditions of theistic hijack of the divine and hollow material inducements keep the new generation moving in line through stick and carrot diplomacy. This story germinates as a personal insight that reveals the world as an immersive, utterly alive intrigue, an abundance in absolute contrast to society's thematic tales of scarcity. Science in its broadly disseminated form served as much to obscure the essentially copious nature of existence. Thus, my personal insight completely lacked of a supportive cultural context. It was without a framework to pay it respect. The experience stood as a single elusive signal amid the noisiness of society's distracting institutional stakeholders. It arose as a reprieve from an otherwise endlessly promoted mosaic of abstracted mis-leading contradictions. This aroused my suspicion. The situation smelled of rats.

What ensued was a personal roaming, a search for a meaningful explanation, one that held a place for such an unforgettable glimpse, one nurturing of true nature. Though slowly it became apparent such explanation may not exist. Perhaps nothing of a magnitude less than a culture needed to provide no less than a set of activities through which such a revelation could be re-minded and kept central as a foundation of an informed life. Yet no such supportive culture appeared available within my homeland. Even that deemed alternative, non-mainstream, felt of little practical utility, finding much of its reason in mere opposition to, while appropriating its resources from, the very system it denigrated.

For a being that lives in awareness of its own existence, this was a crisis. This crisis unresolved settled into manifest depression. Over time this depression trained the skill of tolerable solitude and then accumulated a determination to strike out alone. What followed was a journey through exotic cultures revealed as mainly of a familiar materialistic focus, if not more so, if not more entangled and corrupted to that end. There was no relief. Now this crisis found its despair. This despair persuaded to look within, to further examine the role of personal perspectives as a potential source of the problem.

$$\infty$$

The ingestion of a plant's essential oil had served as my original catalyst towards a direct experience of inextricable intimate relationship with that formerly taught to be separate. It had not been previously explained that plants are able to facilitate such revelations. On the contrary, the culture within which I was raised directly opposes liaison with such plant allies by legislating against their cultivation and use, labelling as criminal those who associate with them, even if the purpose for that association is of wholesome development. In this way individuals of sufficient honesty to question, and of sufficient courage to investigate, are, if not careful, stigmatised if not ostracised.

re-membering

The institution of mainstream science begins its own unique contribution to hindrance of assisted epiphanies from its very foundations. Its view of the world as a collection of discrete material components overlooks the essential holistic nature of the living system, no doubt because this understanding remains beyond the reach of the human sensory apparatus and intellect. Though the school of quantum physics has postulated for over a century the qualities of matter are co-created only through the irreducible intimate effect of a relationship with an observer. Here also, stigmatisation is often used as to deter findings that may otherwise serve to undermine the vested interests of convention. The scientific reductionist often belittles exponents of a literal interpretation of quantum mechanical findings, labelling them as irrational and vague, if not as opportunistic narcissists in search of attention. Convenient to the reductionist is that from their perspective, they appear right. For a believer in fragments, fragments are indeed all that is seen. Although this no less emphasises the power of point of view, and thus the pivotal role of the individual mind in establishing the premise upon which all appears to unfold. Amusingly, the reductionist view leaves its adherents with a hard problem. If all is simply energy and matter, then from where does consciousness arise? Some of them suggest consciousness to be an emergent property of the brain, and thus of matter. Though how could this be? Consciousness contains everything. All arises within it, not the other way around.

Perhaps stigma of the greatest consequence arises as a result of the taboos of religious institutions. A by now famous biblical story tells of a man proclaimed as the son of god who paid with his life for the political and social disruption he caused. The plot goes on to report of his name's eventual acclaim and prosperity, and of a church built upon the legacy of his words and deeds. This institution was also faced with a hard problem, namely, if this man is to be recognised as the son of god, then what of all of us? Is he to be an only child? As is widely known, this decision was upheld, and thus no-one else gets to make a similar claim, and the church gets to keep its central authority. Any such claims by other individuals are quickly rebutted as blasphemous or insane. In this way the religion denies and thus obscures the agency of its followers in the creation of their own world. According to this church we are in no part creator. This sets the scene for an eternal repetition of the same tragic story, as if the son shows up again today, he, as anyone, would only be spared condemnation by remaining silent on his essential realisation. In this social context, how could a son of a god ever be positively identified? Is he with us today? Is he you? Is he me? Is he a she? And so it goes on, and on, and on, and on …

Barriers to direct realisation don't end with the psychedelic, scientific and religious. Taboos appear to be an inbuilt feature of all ideologies. As a further example, the well documented incarceration of intelligentsia and burning of books is a common early strategy of incoming communist regimes. It appears the general role of ideological taboo is to exclude any influence that may otherwise contribute to the demise of the ideology, regardless of the justification.

∞

Granted an upbringing founded upon the scientific belief we exist as members of an animal kingdom, as a type of primate, in a universe constituted otherwise almost entirely of lifeless rocks, and the hangover of a religious belief in an all-powerful creator of a cosmos into which we were born as some kind of misfitting, non-divine entities, we are sent out to find our way.

Within the modernised version of this space, we are bombarded by a broadcast media providing never-ending bad news primarily centred on themes of war, disaster and disease. Amid this fearful atmosphere, the business sector preys upon the understandable normalised feelings of impotence within the populous by suggesting power may be bought back by instalment through the acquisition of products such as fitness and health programmes, special diets, fashion items, cosmetics, surgery makeover, self-help literature; or alternatively the consumer may seek vicarious triumph through identification with celebrities, effectively through watching other people live their lives; or escape as an avatar of endless lives of zero consequence within the digital realm; or find distraction through soothing, numbing drugs, or through the oral ingestion of all manner of unhealthy substance. It is difficult to think of a sector of our human potential upon which at least an attempt has not been made on its colonisation.

What's further misleading to the unsuspecting is an economic system that boasts its success based upon the consuming behaviour of a community trained to feel in lack. The greater the sense of not being enough within the individual, the greater the sense of distance from wholesomeness, the greater the wants and addictions, the greater the spending on placebos, and the better the economic balance sheet.

Through decades of mandatory education, the youth are not only trained towards serving the perpetuation of society's intransigent institutions, and thus unaided in self-fulfilment, they are also rendered socially challenged, poorly placed for the purposes of communicating personal concerns born of this very dilemma. The youth are pressured into conformity, and even if the odd individual finds the courage to bravely discount such treatment, of what and how are they to speak? Beyond the limitations of conversational taboo relating to topics of most gravity, beyond the looming backlash of the resentful hordes, there lies further challenges within the conversational setting.

There exists scant encouragement towards sincere expression, rendering authentic discourse regarding heart-felt concerns difficult to impossible.

re-membering

The cultural conversation is adversarial by nature. It is polarising in its insistence an opinion is either right or wrong. It is without the patience required to entertain necessarily sophisticated ideas on complex issues. Individuals are not trained in simply holding space for others to explore their own thoughts and feelings. There is little support offered in assisting others to develop their perspectives regardless of their orientation. The intolerance towards dissenting views breeds fear of being different. Further, expressions of strong emotion are commonly seen as a sign of weakness. The conversational culture is summarily intimidating, frustrating, unsatisfying and as a consequence, selectively engaged, and often avoided. It leads to a surrender into group think for many and alienation for a not so insignificant number.

In the situation of social engagement, there are also problems embedded within the language itself. Many of the most important of definitions have been side-lined through years of mis-appropriation, words captured through the clever manoeuvrings of the vigilant opportunist that is the market place. There is the diminution of love's power in the term's often manipulative re-purposing within the spheres of community, family and romantic engagement. The notion of respect has immeasurable value in describing the will to honour a source of beneficial learning, yet nothing rings so disrespectful as to hear this word threateningly used in an attempt to coerce the weak to blindly accommodate another's narrow self-interest. Without re-sent-ment there would be no catharsis, though in its monopolising mis-identification as a motivation for worldly action, resentment is characterised solely as an agent of potential destructive consequence. I know nothing more indicative of the transcendent than the notion of god-liness, yet nothing so misleading as to define the divine as a quality that dwells external to the essence of every individual. I know nothing more condescending as to dismissively label as spiritual or philosophical those who speak simply and honestly of their direct and very real experience to those who live in fear of looking beyond their own pretence. And then there's the common confusion of the intuitive nature of empathy with the often-destructive projected confusion of sympathy.

In order for a conversation of value to proceed, consensus must first be found on what terms actually mean.

It is not surprising healthy guidance is hard to find. Social groups tend to coalesce and develop from schoolyard allegiances, within religious affiliations, through sports club patriotism, among workplace colleagues, or around choices of addiction. All were brought up similarly within materialistic possessive dogmas, in the absence of wise counsel, reared as to not question external authority, and thus led away from the development of autonomous intelligence, and thus discouraged from the constructively imaginative, the co-operatively integrated, and ultimately, the wholesome.

The accumulative impact of the normal upbringing not only leaves individuals in neglect of the tools of navigation required for a uniquely upstanding life, it also fundamentally challenges attempts at a healthy simple life, inhibiting the alignment of genuine inspiration with the action of fulfilment. This has been my consistent experience.

From the end of my school days, from the time I first became concerned regarding my life and its meaning, this has been my consistent experience - from the adult demands for my childhood compliance through the threat of physical punishment; in my classmate's denigration and making mockery of any attempt at honest expression of thoughts, feelings or opinions; in traveller's appearing to settle for mere distraction over authentic foreign cultural engagement; monks seemingly going through mere customary motion; the religious claims theirs is the one and only; activists opting for antagonistic tribalism over universal co-operation; scientists insisting upon personal perspectives as if universal facts; party-goers shutting down rather than opening up; to the shallow state of fellowship, solidarity and intimacy within and between the genders - in summary, individuals maintaining obstacles to their own and other's development rather than aiding, or at least not hindering. This has been my consistent experience.

∞

This predicament may be conveniently pondered through the lens of evolution. That is to say, these are the circumstances from which we have emerged, circumstances within which we have fought competitively, aggravated by immeasurably broad external challenges. Though now our complicity is self-evident. It is us that maintain our array of entrained beliefs and behaviours without question, colluding through our own wilful ignore-ance.

Of course, the situation is not the same as if a matter of inconsequential choice. For most, the greater priority remains personal survival, and this is inextricably tied to maintaining a place within the community and thus within its theatre. This survival impulse is carried through the generations, forming a significant factor of our embodiment and identity before we have even the rudiments of an ability to think for ourselves. Thus, in the absence of a later uncompromising concern for what is actually true, our social character and its internalised image remains a trap, indeed the only trap.

On the surface, it certainly appears easier to perpetuate a life of well-rehearsed unconscious behaviours born of such prolonged re-inforced conditioning, especially where these behaviours are further indirectly accustomed, if not co-erced, through the on-going demands for consistency within the peer group. It especially appears easier when behaviours summarily amount to a placating pseudo-self if this finds some success in appeasing disharmony or avoiding controversy within social environments that maintain a consistent pressure to conform.

The agreeable personality type is thus common not because of agreement, rather due to the ever-looming threat of the consequences of dis-agreement. For those of this character, unconventional verbalisations remain of questionable utility, potentially undermining to the survival strategy that is the insignificant figure. Those of such character won't much bother, will receive little sincere attention, will exist as a compliant citizen regardless of the social and political surrounds.

Yet the price paid for this survival strategy is surely too great. In the absence of a value placed upon a heart of a will to express, we not only remain hostage to the role played as the victim of endless circumstance, we also arrest our development.

The strategy appears ill-informed, as even for those who simply claim a desire for a peaceful life, equally there are no assurances. Anomalies necessarily persist within the cultural matrix, no less because incongruences persist within the very ideologies to which such mainstream frameworks owe their allegiance, upon which common social strategies and emergent group dynamics rely for their vindication. Component ideological concepts, due to their abstract nature, remain shallow, intolerant of close scrutiny. The interpretation placed upon even the most common of notions such as equality, justice and rights struggle to provide a consistent and uniform protection amid the rough and tumble of the ancient embodied drives and dis-positions active within the mammalian herd.

Thus, social and political frameworks offer little more than a means to a floating community order, a fragile safe haven within an otherwise fickle crowd, lubricated through the currency of rehearsed platitudes or even cynicisms. The milieu ebbs and flows on a shifting foundation of consensus for the sake of consensus, for the sake of moving in unison.

Beyond any argument regarding acceptable compromise for the purpose of maintaining a place within the social group, there exists further potential for tension emergent from this tendency to conform. A community of relatively strong internal consistency is more likely to experience antagonism upon encountering groups of differing persuasion within the broader population. People conditioned within a so-called democratic narrative commonly take issue with people brought up within a so-called socialist narrative and vice versa, the religious ideologue sees heathens, the scientific ideologue has little time for the irrational.

Further, the common inclination to avoid discomfort renders the entire social group somewhat predictable, and thus remains a key enabling factor for those inevitable external authoritative manipulations. The cumulative result of this tendency is an en masse acquiescence, essentially sustaining a societal class ostensibly enslaved to goals impersonal of design and habitually suggestible through a relentless memetic urging and persuading that all is for the best.

As the entire societal dynamic plays out through an exchange of rehearsed words, actions and omissions, the general tone remains disingenuous, and thus not of an internal moral compass. Within this atmosphere persuasion takes the form of summary dictates framed in terms of the reigning dogma and distracted from reference to genuine feeling. This disconnect disables empathic connection. As a consequence people leave themselves vulnerable to extremes; and granted the pre-conditions, to mass hysteria; and in that situation, are capable of untold atrocity.

And all the while, within the total population of seemingly diverse communities and classes, amid all the push and pull, each individual contains much more in common than is generally understood - sharing of the same unitary consciousness, embodied of the same elemental earth, similarly projecting of a socialised mind frame, similarly desiring of belonging, executing from within the same potential, viewing all on behalf of the very same essence, albeit through separate pairs of eyes.

∞

Knowledge of our innate similarities runs counter to our initial divisive indoctrinations. We all start out along the lines of a shared native ideology. Newborns arrive without a notion, without any idea, without even a sense of separation. This oceanic feeling of infancy is well documented. Early parental intimacy begins the honing of senses and emotions. During this phase preferences and discriminations emerge. These are further imbued with low resolution feelings of an outside world of meaning tempered through the formal and informal influence of the domestic culture.

With the formation of a personal caricature, an assumed self as a subject to which events appear to happen, the non-dual ground of being is dis-membered. Of this pivotal moment there is no memory as we know memory to be. Memory only begins to function once the premise of duality has been established. The emergent, notional self proceeds to develop as a con-sequence of all that subsequently arises, governing perceptions, and in so doing, influencing outcomes.

In this way, all that appears to happen is of the nature of an artifice - to think a specific phenomenon is of a certain character is not totally incorrect, though to think the nature of this something exists separate from the self's actioning is ignorant. This moment to moment self and the world of meaning within which it finds its image is continually born and re-born of and as such integral deceptions.

re-membering

∞

It is commonplace to claim conspiracy upon epiphany's revelation of the deceit that, until that waking moment, equated conditioned perspectives with objective truths. It is easy to feel let down upon the re-cognition of that previously mis-taken for qualities of something of an independent, worldly existence. However, this reaction is unhelpful. Every culture necessarily inculcates stories that define the people's place. Without them there would be no shared meaning through which to co-operate, no foundation upon which to exchange, no structure through which we secure our continued survival. There would be no society.

Functionally, all ideologies present within the context of a culture's historical becoming and thus constitute no less a relic of past utility. In this context, all worldly phenomena exist beyond a need for judgment. Existence is its own undeniable meaning. The presence of a church speaks volumes, as does a microscope, a telephone, a suit, or a mini-skirt.

Conducting a hunt for a scapegoat is anyway unreasonable. This merely perpetuates otherwise avoidable suffering for all concerned. No-one could ever force us to feel, think, say or do anything. To vengefully persist is to dishonour the free will which we always embodied though only later fathom in its reach.

History, though convenient to its writers, still provides adequate inference into how we got here in terms of our cultural evolution. Large societies only arise through the advent of institutions that govern the many. As a matter of course these institutions are administered, not through the wisdom that inspired them, eventually not even by their founders, but by their followers.

To raise religion for the purpose of example, Buddha was not a Buddhist, Jesus was never a Christian. The institutional lineages that grow from the legacy of such historical or mythical figures tend away from the original knowledge that inspired them simply because those embodying of this knowledge are no longer around. In the absence of direct personal insight, subsequent institutional authorities and their adherents default to the idolatry of the original inspiring figure considered of unique and mysterious power, becoming identified with an exaggerated, externalised image meant to represent the outer physical form of someone whose relevance has nothing to do with that outer physical form. All the while those within the congregation continue to operate out of innate blind self-interest, though now motivating and expanding their actions based upon a belief engendered within the community of their uniquely superior moral certitude.

∞

Despite this common group behavioural tendency, lines of transmission of essential wisdom have, as yet, not all been broken, at least not in this epoch. It may still be divined. Within the play of the unfettered imagination, a perfection may still be excavated and pieced together from the ruins of most historical legacies.

In continuing with the religious analogy, it requires a single act of good faith to give a sincere and respectful nod to biblical stories of the birth of self-consciousness, that defining quality of humanity, and its transcendence, resurrection, through the renouncing of the personal, in existing beyond the self as a mere idea and as an outstanding central concern. Though this does not justify the elevation of any story to the exclusion of other stories, it does not make its adherents exclusively special, it appoints no external authority or saviour, offloads not a single worldly responsibility, constitutes no means to a single worldly end.

For those of us without religious leanings, perhaps this may be expressed more tastefully in terms of a rational or pragmatic psychology. That is to say, the way to be free of the tyranny of unconscious ideological possessions is to become conscious in relationship to them. And to observe them is to become conscious of them, as again, that which can be observed is simultaneously seen as not forming a necessary part of the observer.

In this way, integrity is maintained through an on-going awareness of the lenses through which we co-create worlds. And to respect them is to view individual perspectives as arising from among a countless potential many, as single temporary contexts for feelings, emotions, thoughts, words and actions to have their time and place, a point of view to thank and let go when seen as no longer of value.

It is through consciousness that we may discover a life that burgeons with immaculate reflections upon the stage of the imagination, while simultaneously reminding of who or what is truly served and of service.

∞

re-membering

There is no substitute for grounded awareness. Experience otherwise continues to unfold in reflection of that mindscape moulded since the very earliest days of infancy, re-enforcing a latent array of fragmentary dis-harmonious impulses. The unconscious life continues to re-act, feeding into an assortment of worldly scenarios much like the actions of ragtag squatters within the premises of the absentee landlord. Even though constituted of such a flickering array of piecemeal projections, the experience of such a mind still remains irresponsibly misidentified by the unquestioning host. Perceptions remain indistinguishable from attributes of an external world. To the unconscious individual this appears not as a matter of choice, but as a reality.

Whether by intention or accident, the foundation of a fulfilling life is initially re-dis-covered by seeing through earlier conditioning, and beyond re-dis-covery, by setting forth upon the non-dual ground. There is no need for confusion. This ground is unmistakable. The one and only - unmistakable. Here exists life. This is life without death and thus without such concern. This is omni-presence life, neither here nor there.

For the first time all makes sense. It is crystal clear that all arises within. It is crystal clear that all that arises is of intimate connection and relevance. It is thus implicit, and consequently experienced, that will remains the most powerful of influences, and that will, when motivated through genuine inspiration and desire, facilitated through the power of the imagination, expresses its fulfilment.

Life for all proceeds in accordance with the same universal principles. The only difference between individuals is that most appear to experience the products of the imagination without being conscious of their true nature. For these people, what is experienced is something that appears to happen to them. Though this is not the case. Personal observation reveals this. And in setting such unconscious perspectives free, a blank canvas is revealed, a canvas upon which now innovative vistas may be lavished in accordance with heart's desire. If I know anything, it is this.

re-membering

I had previously been re-membered of existence as a non-dual ground comprising of the potential for all possible appearances of discrete phenomena. I was re-minded of the inherent polarity within all that arises from this ground as subjective experience, within all personal meaning.

Post-reminder, my initial inspired activities had not called upon grand new visions. My activist and community service predilections had been incubating since my youth, and executed through personal characterisations largely contiguous of that same period. My worldly fashion endured without significant re-invention, and thus without provoking the turning out of pockets that may otherwise accompany the disrobing of previous apparel. This was before sexual exploration became the priority.

A highlighting of personal dysfunction within the sphere of intimate female relations brought to the surface unconscious counter-productive beliefs, leading to their release. My ensuant experiences progressively shed light on more general areas of less than optimal functioning. Such is the influence and impact of sexual possibility throughout the broader concerns of the sexually reproducing organism.

It was through the establishment of a useful innovative framework towards physical intimacy I realised the nature and pivotal importance of serviceable frames in general. In a life inspired of a specific activity, maintaining a straightforward awareness is obviously not enough. Beyond the eschewing of counter-productive mind arisings, it made sense a suitable preparation and plan of engagement be entrained, no different than as for an archer, mechanic, priest or stripper.

This exploration ultimately had less specifically to do with sex or women. It brought me to a threshold from which I am able to proceed with the integrating of all that I am, bringing my movement within the world to a more complete dynamic wholesomeness. It exposed so much more of what is available within the self. This adventure just as much came to focus on growing into fullness, freeing up all aspects of the incarnated bodily vehicle, this means to experience, providing a training towards a buoyant upstanding amid greater extremes of activity.

∞

Is there any limit to what may be accomplished through heart-felt endeavour? Is there anything we cannot embody and have mirrored back as that which we desire? Realising oneself as the centre of one's own universe reveals quite the potential for adventure.

In regard of this seemingly endless possibility, it makes relative sense to self-impose a detailed spatial and temporal limitation to keep things manageable. Painting and playing out the victim arguably occupies close to one extreme of this limitation gradient, performing the character which explains away any good reason for wilful engagement in novel activity. The other extreme appears more as a vanishing point, that of a freedom indescribable by its very nature.

Is this not a grand creative project? It would be hard to find agreement among the aforementioned, those who sport the badge of victimhood, the creators of perhaps the most outstanding of personal sleight-of-hand building projects, that of a collaboration towards an imposed set of barriers in the service of excuse. Though this strategy as much brims with the potential for innovation as any other. Those who accuse worldly events without admission of complicity remain creatively busy, contributing to the affirmation of that deemed inappropriate, unacceptable or intolerable through their very opposition. This world's generous acceptance of all such co-operative creation is reflected in its relatively unlimited capacity for homely accommodation.

In the general context of desire's exploration, even the unconscious mind finds its perfect utility, its own contribution to the functionality of limitation. The unconscious hides away that which may otherwise deter, that which may otherwise undermine the will to venture. Though upon any given journey towards novelty, the unrelenting traveller invariably confronts the unconscious in a piecemeal re-dis-covery of that long forgotten, on the way to experiencing that previously known to perhaps no-one, perhaps no-where, perhaps never, perhaps as part of a truly universal expansion.

As much as the many declare aspirations beyond limitation, as much as the many proclaim aspiration towards the freedom end of the spectrum, it is surely not freedom to which almost all of these many are referring. Freedom is not forever sipped through a seaside straw. Experience recognises the almost archetypal luxuriating vista as at best an abstracted snapshot of a vacation scenario arrived at beyond a prerequisite challenging ascent. The path towards it takes the form of a transformation arc, though of a design uniquely shaped, resourced by the energy of catharsis, repurposed towards the realisation of that novel spectacle. The destination becomes temporarily accessible only for those who have made the necessary sacrifices.

re-membering

For those who truly possess an uncompromising hunger for the realisation of their full potential, for those who sense an illumination that awaits beyond a finite path, within and beyond this desire and its call abides the mother of all freedom, the eternal emancipating moment. She resides in the background and within the very fabric of all worldly events. She hides in plain sight when viewed as and through the complex prism of personal perspectives. As such, she does not exist for the purpose of undermining worldly authority, nor to oppose the relevance of belief, nor to disapprove of conventional facts. She simply rests in her maternity, birthing all without favour. Her door is always open, her home always a welcome place. Indeed this is the only true home, as it is only here residents may rest in complete relaxation, abide beyond all confusion, exist without pre-tension, be-come indistinguishable from the atmosphere that permeates this dwelling.

This too may be hard to believe, more difficult as it may be to recall the circumstances of a tree's beginnings when perched far out on its high limb. Though when circumstances press for a re-location from lofty heights to safe ground, and fear grips on regarding the distance between, the approach remains the same. A focused enjoyment of every descending hold makes nothing of conceptual scenarios nor judgments, remains respecting of all contributions known to existence, makes nothing more of what is than what is. The arising resistance is informative in passing, reminding this project of that which does not serve. The arising reluctance is telling, reminding this project of that which exists as mere dis-traction.

The indirect community, civilisational and worldly benefits of feet on the ground cannot be overstated. While out on a limb, action tends to serve short term individual survival and thus cares little for the consequences. In contrast, the re-membering of our foundational non-dual, non-discriminant nature instantly refreshes our intimate familiarity within the ineffable, and thus by default re-solves any previously held tensions with branches of ideology and the tribes that rest upon them. The same re-membering re-vitalises a scientific understanding of acts and consequences within the world through a wholly direct seeing, providing a breathing ecological context to the otherwise incisory surgical psychopathy of mere abstract theory, its data, mathematical interpretations and wanton applications.

The summary result of feet on the ground is the lifting of ignore-ance and its unavoidable suffering, suffering to self, to others, to nature in general. The result transcends the re-actionary rough justice of the prisoner of conscience and its institutional counterpart present within systems of law. The result forms the basis of a universal jurisprudence, one activated not of ideas but of true relationship, one generated of, and as a re-membering, from the ground up.

re-membering

*sincerely contemplate for a full moment
that referenced as apparent worldly experience as in truth
that which is mind*

*is not that proclaimed as the important details of a life
primarily the sundry of thoughts, feelings, perceptions, of imaginings?*

for a dedicated moment look, …………………………

*and then if acknowledged to be true, hold that viewing position,
like a thread,*

*hold it as simply possible for that which is inside self,
and not outside world*

re-membering

continuing in this respect constitutes a reclaiming
of the long-evacuated seat,

feel into the intuition of this chair's accommodation,

appreciate without effort its fabric born of timeless nature,

its provision of evolution's granting, humanity's lineage,
and society's accommodation,

its reference through the auspices of ancient sages and contemporary
far-reaching technology

beyond seeing all relevant as of thinking, feeling, perceiving, imagining,

let go of that which is old and not of service,

resume your place as the creator, as the righteous cause,

dream the dream of the dreamer for the dreamee,

it is not difficult, nor is it easy

create to the heart's content, it is your true nature,
it is who you are,

you're doing it anyway

re-membering

Glossary of additional lost meanings

condescending	to go down together; any attitude to other that services a perspective of mutually being lesser than respectfully honoured
confidence	con-fide-ence, to trust in yourself totally, as opposed to arrogant posturing
divine	the as yet undiscovered, more essential self, inseparable from other
holy	wholly
in-formation	that which provides the building blocks of the mind's imagery and projection
realisation	to realise; the quality of seeing in actuality; often confused with abstract conceptual understanding
sacred	what you are, unquestioningly, and thus a measure through which to treat the self devotionally, this is maintained through conscious awareness

Made in the USA
Columbia, SC
09 February 2024

52de261f-3ff4-4891-a687-759b570fe27dR02